WALKING THE SUNSET HOME

WALKING THE SUNSET HOME

POEMS

JOHN E. SIMONDS

atmosphere press

For RBS,
a source of life and ideas for many,
with love and aloha
to all our families,
and caring friends,
past and present,
here and gone

Preface

This is my fourth book of poems. As the title suggests, it continues late-in-life views on a range of topics—weighty, light and mysterious—that caught my attention in recent times.

Writing with wonder about what's ahead is part of the theme, but so also is re-exploring the past. How yesterday's events and curious images light the way from memory's backdrop extends the collection's span.

Picture a striding writer scribbling old visions and current insights, racing the days remaining to pursue new understandings of then and now with an eye on twilight's clock, nature's reality ticktock.

Some pieces reflect the life of a journalist-witness to national events dating back to the 1950s. Others show a player in personal moments of life's bright, strange and surprising journey in a world still evolving from one century into the next.

Water—the ever-present Pacific, a childhood Hudson, lakes and rivers elsewhere—surfaces as another thematic link in the life of a writer who has been a flood-zone dweller for nearly a half-century.

Poems relating to health and illness, touching on family issues and stress of careers, share influence with pieces on backyard birds and other animal life, near and far.

Readers who've browsed previous books, *Waves from a Time-Zoned Brain* (2009), *Footnotes to the Sun* (2015), and *In a Roundabout Way* (2021) may have noted earlier eclectic reflections on life then and now in Hawai'i and elsewhere.

Pandemia with its stress and strategies shaped the creative effort that went into this book. The miracle of Zooming enabled a sharing of work with distant groups after local in-person gatherings closed.

Ekphrastic artwork and other prompts spurred responses to pictures and phrases, not always about the objects or words themselves but remote inklings and conceits unleashed by viewing them, poetic connections deeply secluded or hiding in brain sight.

Thanks to all who've shared in these motivating on-line exchanges and readings that kept worded ideas flowing at a time when so much else stopped. Deadline tension of preparing for screens elsewhere has worked well to link us with the elusive passcodes of our own poetic identities.

Mahalo to all who helped guide me on the way toward whatever horizon awaits.

John E. Simonds
Honolulu, Hawai'i 2023

Table of Contents

Connecting the Curated Dots:
Some Assembly Required

Other Creatures, Other Lives

At the Corner of Good Times and Twilight:
The Angels Are in the Details

CURRENT MOMENTS AND OTHER SHOCKS

Another Round in the Chamber

Each national disease that occupies
our revolving collective attention
leaves us waiting outside the action
in quarantine mode from immediate care,
hoping in frieze for something to happen
to unjam the lock from the load that links
hospital hearts to bank-account minds,
freeing the advance of delivery
while others adjust their masks
to shield against loss of the hard-won,
speaking out to control the unwanted,
to filibuster infection that accepts no yield
in trajecting death bursts of priority floor moves
against ailing forces that fill capital beds
with terminal causes and cries to make care
of the body guilt-free and cost-free for all,
to let in the needy, hold back the angry,
liquefy the process of words to soften the facts.
Where *reconciliation* has a language of its own,
unachievable among clashing people,
but words of art enabling work-around and carve-out,
spawning legislative life in a protected loophole
where one more than half is enough.

Let the armed aim to arm their armies
to encourage the dead to bury their own,
while awaiting cures to be approved
for sidewalk dwellers whose rainbows
end where concrete meets chain link,

and on border roads without direction,
walls and fences merging with no end in sight.
Who gets to live on which side of the river,
the cinder-block walls, or the spur-line tracks?
How far do we aid the hopes of freedom
caught in a hostile pinch with lethal neighbors
immune to the droning pressures for truce?
Vague dreams of an elder surviving mind
see alternate chaos rotating ideas in deadlock,
conveying the hope of unfinished life
propelled by the shaky needs of successive
senior agendas with uneven success:
—*guns and butter, blood and treasure,*
hearts and minds, people to people,
containment, territorial imperatives,
captive nations, massive retaliation,
agonizing reappraisal, thinking the unthinkable,
mutual self-destruction, balance of terror,
anti-missile missiles, eyeball to eyeball,
dirty little back alley fights that let us sleep.

How slogans of passing policy-mongers
bounce around in the memory
like empty shells ejecting
from a smoking breech,
yielding endless casings
of empty metal clanking
wildly about in untouchable heat,
as though conclusion's reach
outflanks the present's grasp to act,
extending sights toward a range
of every session's unmet targets,

as lives bleed out on boundaries
corralled by tangled wire
and the smoke of burning dirt.

Truth of the Matter

Is truth in the eye of the beholden
or in the <u>view</u> of a master's gaze?
Versions of it appear in pupils we trust,
learning, aging, staring at us directly.
Had Einstein lived more light years,
he might have developed a theory
of truth as a relative concept,
linking time and atomized details,
as in, "What did we know, and when
did we know it?"
Seeing through the protective
half-truth foliage of human nature,
we part the leafy lenses to read
how we balanced the facts of today,
displaying them in customized array.
Would the master's formula go something like:
T (as in truth) =Facts+Hopes+Needs
or T=Evidence-Doubts+Popular Belief.

In everyday terms, I tell you the house I'm selling
offers a brilliant sunrise view. True enough..
But I omit to remind the setting sun dies
in early shadows of the ridge behind.
How many such solar facts
does the standard of truth require?
Has truth become a team sport?
We field our facts vs. you furnish doubts.
The need, the hope, the popular faiths,
get folded, apart and together at once,

like greens in a suburb of salads,
held together by oil and vinegar,
seasoned to taste, a yin-and-yang combo
of sharing in piecemeal honesty.

How often have we camouflaged truth
in shaded rays, selectively lensing
adjusted measures of a light that fit?
What heals and feeds us could be free,
but the providing has its costs.
Truth's a better gift when its price tag shows.
Consider the leaves as equation models,
eating C and emitting O,
a wreathing of vital exchange
that puts a good look on truth,
saving the face of the science behind it.

China Seminars

Guests around the table talk and ponder,
some seem younger, but traveled and wiser
in ways our side of the world knows best,
cheering programs, projects and plans.

But old China hands are also apparent,
sharing sweet-sour storied regimes,
triumph and travail to flavor the menu,
salting the air with a grayness of wisdom.

All speak of places they've studied
and served at work for nation and self
with knowing nods of recognition,
news of where old colleagues were last seen.

They talk of Tiananmen, the Great Wall, Silk Road,
Mao and his great leaps forward,
the vanishing flight of Lin Piao,
Tibet and Hong Kong, Taiwan and tariffs.

Consider China's business eruption,
pouring new roads to advance the Third-World
and flowing "frenemy" US loans in the trillions,
a debt guests understand but rarely mention.

People we watch may be gone or still plotting
their spreading or shrinking spheres of sway.
The talk drifts to shadowy vignettes
and back to nuanced nods of awareness…

...of trends perceived but not stated
from semesters of global perusal
or missions unspoken, still at work
in the world-watch of adventured ambition.

Was Zhou en Lai a really good guy?
How did Deng Xiaoping succeed without titles?
Was the time of Li Peng a truly bad thing?
Does Xi Jinping want to be king?

Waiters delivers hot bowls
faster than people can speak.
We slide them around a rotating disc
serving ten at each white-clothed table.

Let 10,000 steaming platters bloom!
Watch their nine-course magic blossom,
careful not to bump our drinking glasses,
won ton cups and dipper handles.

Fish soup, beef-broccoli, ginger-chicken,
mounded rice, beans in gravy, lemon chicken,
char siu bao and other incoming dishes
arrive in fragrant flights of noontime landings.

The intensity of circular lunch
ladles and stirs the continued talk,
excited by food or serene in the moment,
with chopsticks and spoons at 360°.

That quieter side of the table speaks
of emeritus service, alien detachment,
diplomatic nostalgia, cocktails of suspicion
sipped on terraces of intrigue at sunset.

At meals for visiting speakers
comments seem aimed at displaying
the knowledge of askers and *bonhomie*
hinting at been there, done that too.

"As I'm sure you recall
 from our days in the past…"
We pray for the blunt host to blurt,
"What is your question?"

Lunch ends, as the lingering learneds
and leaving listeners sort themselves out
extending hails, farewells and aloha
to the scraping sounds of close chairs.

Personal needs intrude for patient use
by guests bursting with global substance
to clarify their issues in a single-stall restroom,
a measure of urgent respect among those at all levels.

Taking Privacy Public

Life begins between borders
from the instant we start
to the time we arrive
puzzled by which door to open
in walled portals of chance,
our bold eyes hiding
hope's fears behind masks
as required among creatures of choice.

Life entwines windows of law:
open-carry, have a baby, change
your ways of bringing forth
by redesigning gender parts;
embrace a new menagerie,
lion's head, curled lizard, squid aspread,
reminders of jungle, desert, sea,
of routes we've crossed to get here.

Life dares the border patrol
to strip search for contraband
conceived and borne past
the trimester checkpoint,
as authority inserts its eminence
into our secret domain to ask
how much life are we hauling
inside our personal carry-on?

Life takes form in our curious vault,
compared by some to the branching
head of a long-horned steer
in its outline, an evolving cradle
and common berth of origin for all,
rarely portrayed, even in embryo scans.
The law seeks us out at the border,
claiming its rights of adverse possession.

Life has made fun of how little we know
of ourselves and our inner controls.
A friend enjoyed cocktail joking that
he was an "amateur gynecologist."
His blank face and raised brows
made even women guests laugh.
In the '80s, wine and nonsense
went well with reception chatter.

Life now anoints many such amateurs,
men in robes making much the same claim,
while we at the edges of legal existence,
sense the reach of more strangers in power,
probing our personal love compartments,
stretching a party-line spoof into a platform
of chambers, where religions have bloomed
and families produced on demand.

Life extradites choice from its desperate zones,
where greeting new births can be chancy
and brief as the pairings that formed them.
Organs beyond plain sight, not a topic for dinner,
except among nurses who've labored

on both sides of the forceps and hands,
grasping at separate life from the pain of its giving,
body parts yielding loss from the sum of their hopes.

We Need to Talk

As tired as I am of each weary cliché,
I have to conclude at the end of the day
it is what it is, and what can I say?
Things happen for a reason.
There's something to be said for that,
whatever the season.
Yatta yatta yatta…
What goes around comes around,
do what you may,
or look the other way.
Make no mistake,
and don't get me wrong.
You asked about optics?
So, what would that look like?
It's not OK. OK?
OK, have it your way.
In what world is what you say
ever going to be OK?
No way, or so you say,
a game-changing play.
We're backing away,
dialing back to the day
before toxic fray
conflated to weaponize
false equivalents on display,
making less room to play
with only binary options to weigh.
Whaddayamean?…Whaddabout?!
It's complicated.

Make it all go away.
Hello! Are you even listening?
You should hear yourself say
what you're saying today.
When did it become OK
to stockpile clichés
for the overflow day
when outpouring them all
could wash the slate clean
and channel the way
for new waves of clichés.
Backwater the old to a phase,
you might say,
past their old fields of play
which, oh, by the way,
still need to be leveled.
It's now a new day,
but words that still work
remain here to stay.
No need to ask, "Are you OK?"
Because I think I'm hearing you say,
"For words without end
let us pray." Amen.
Free your thoughts, as we speak,
and more to the point,
be plainly direct as a bird.
Go forth to love and serve the word.
Look around you for more to be heard,
just a few housekeeping notes
without favor or fear.
We're awaiting the votes
while the jury's still out

to make things perfectly clear.
Our world's round, not flat,
and, having said that,
are we done here?

Halls of Justice

Steps to the crystal courthouse
flank a balanced display of purple and green
plants, a floral greeting to equity's temple,
its welcoming archway a cross
between a horseshoe magnet drawing all in
and a restraining collar to hold life in place.
Three months ago someone's food caught fire
while cooking on the seventh floor,
sparking a smoky exodus of courthouse
workers in a new twist of the "All Rise" command,
dozens fleeing through glass doors
into the street front plaza, two-stepping
to safety in time with the siren rhythms.
Glad that all survived, one still might sneer
it was the quickest action seen there in too long.
Justice delayed is justice defined
in the world of the castle-like courthouse.
Commissioners tell us no one's working,
as the unmet backlog flowers
like the shrubs in the garden out front.
Judges blame it on the DA's testing,
drugs and mental screening of defendants and parolees.
The DA says there is no backlog,
blames the Covid cautions for delays.
Others urge electric anklets to free
imprisoned inmates from their crowded cells.
But gridlock runs this game of right and wrong.
Justice delayed is justice du jour.
The temple bears the name of a pillar

of the ruling party, fond of the storied oath
He governs best who governs least, a motto
whose spirit echoes wide in the land.
In this court winners of life are elusive.
Five cops were shot while having their coffee.
How was their killer dealt with, their families supported?
A quiet man was killed in his own apartment,
mistakenly thought to be her place
by the drunken cop who shot him.
Bad blood on both sides of the badge
breaks out every day, good guys losing
in churches and schools, crowds living in danger.
Does Lady Justice have enough scales
to weigh all the grief, while directing
the traffic in docket detritus.
The temple invites our look up to the law,
to think of its flowers as blossoms of hope,
not as burial beds for its failures.
Does the courthouse welcome with action
or merely share time with us in its hallways,
armed with the law, but waiting for orders?

HR Stands for Hugging Rules

Your Human Resources Department is all in favor of love,
of expressions of hope and sympathy,
but wants to be sure we're all together on this,
together, that is, in a professional way,
one consistent with our products
and the message we share with each other.

Since the company relaxed its rules
on face masks and distance,
reports have reached our desk concerning
an outbreak of hugging
and closer embracing
in the midst of the workplace.

Several employees have said
this affection pandemic
brings them discomfort,
feelings of unwanted witness
to employee close-contact
in ways that offend and invade.

This is a reminder of long-standing
company policies against
prolonged touching of others,
with or without their permission,
and also public displays of proximity
making others feel marginalized...

...objectified, or victims of microagression,
all to be dealt with precisely
in this HR rule-book refresher,
updated in light of changes
in workplace behavior: Hugging
in modified form will continue.

To enhance safe spontaneity,
staffers should fill out the
form provided to declare their
availability for such unplanned
moments when emotion prompts
action that brings two or more together.

Appropriate positioning requires
that arms should embrace shoulders
or possibly upper back zones,
with hands six inches above waists
at all times. Heads may touch,
lips out of sight and preferably closed.

Restrooms and supply closets
are inappropriate for hugging.
Ideally, embraces should occur
in full view, witnessed by persons
of two or more genders,
one of whom may be a timekeeper.

Photos may be taken
to document personnel records
but not to be sold on social media.
Reasons for hugging have grown
in today's world for occasions
to congratulate or share sorrow.

Celebrations·should·be limited
to promotions, weddings, graduations,
family rites of passage and other good news.
Bereavement and other sympathy hugs
should observe limits to keep the day light.
Quotas of mourning events are imposed.

Deaths from old age and nature
allow a limit of two daily; tragic passings get more.
Auto accident deaths have a limit of three,,
as do those from Pandemic and other diseases.
Losses of those from firearms fall outside
the quotas, beyond the scope of this office.

We also have heard from the great unhugged,
those feeling left out of body engagement.
Our collective bargaining contract says
this is a benefit all must share, and we will.
Please consult HR's directory; sign-up to show
your outreach for hugging inclusion.

Loose Change

We seem to be leaving our coins behind
a bit like we did to weigh down the dollars
we put on the table as tips.
Notice they no longer live in our pockets
or return in the form of change.
Yet it seems all about change,
evolving new ways of trade,
metal to paper to plastic
with silver, nickel and copper,
once shiny discs and circles of value
now rounded out in gifts to the needy,
so purchase receipts come out even
with symmetrical comforts
round figures produce.
We still carry coins in our car
to satisfy parking meters,
feed Laundromats and library copy machines,
or make frantic quarterback handoffs
of quick fistfuls of cash
to the sad-faced people with cardboard signs
who wait for us all at the turning-light stop
if we can engage with eye contact,
windows down, quick-money grasp,
like a relay without a baton,
before the green arrow
warns us it's time to move on.
The wielders of help signs want bills,
but we give them hand-me down
fragments of metal worth less

and call it spare change,
not real change, but lower-cost relatives
with the same last name.
Pennies, dimes, nickels and quarters
used to pile up in pig banks and jars.
How strange those levels are lower
and pockets no longer need checking
nor silver for pay phones kept handy.
The coins no longer around
may some day be found
as treasure stored in the ground,
time capsule tokens of how people spent
before coins and the realm of their owners
rolled off in different directions,
heads one way, tails the other.

Living Better through Plastic

Or, The Cosmetics of Currency

Credit cards helped us save face,
when we couldn't find Andy's, Alex's, Abe's
or GW's—who never said, "I cannot tell a lie,
I'm broke," —at home in our billfolds.

New wrinkles in money and crypto
have lifted the profiles of old fiscal outlooks,
draining and cutting our secret pockets of fat.
Feel the scissored edges slicing
past our unrepentant yesterdays,
sprinkling shreds and shards
of names and numbers
into separate sacks of daily rubbish,
curbing landfill puzzle reassemblers.

You might call it plastic surgery,
not the kind that frees your eyes
from aging bags but restores your balance,
quick snips into garbage bags,
springing us to join the dimpled world of Botox flocks.

In days when interest from the cards
was tax-deducted, spending spread like lesions,
metastasizing the indebted
with shadowed eyes from working
night and day to make their payments.

We opted for the punishment of rescue
from the ageless cowboy leader,
movieland smile and sculpted red-brown hair,
a cheery White House spendthrift face
not portrayed on any legal tender—yet.

Old habits return, as illness resurges,
and now new health cards make an Rx co-pay
slide away for another day.
Edge it into the druggist's machine,
and begone are Big Pharma costs
of Atorvastatin and Nifedipine,
Warfarin and Gentamicin,
Tamsulosin and Trulicity,
Rovastatin and Azelastine.

Learning to pronounce them gives a brain boost.
It may not cure but plants an ego-medicated grin
along our science-savvy faces,
as we sign with stylus in the screen box,
showing that as customers of wellness,
we exist and face the future.
Sliding rectangles of faith—
in cards we trust—are still on tap
as cash-flow pills!

Discovery, Diners Club and Amex
with its metal-value cards of upgrade alchemy,
Visa, Capital and Mastercard,
still lend appearances of wealth
in facing down waiters and clerks,
save for such dreaded moments as,

"I'm sorry, Sir, we only take cash,"
or, "Excuse me, Sir. Your card's been declined.
Perhaps you have another that works,"
in a tone implying that maybe
its owner is someone who doesn't.

Aging in a Repetitive World

Unlike its survivors,
our history never grows old.
It changes in the telling,
fades in the forgetting,
leaving its reminders
to mount in museums
and herky-jerk excerpts
of time-marching newsreels,
invading boots and arms in motion.
Voices trained in strident drama,
heraldic narrators in doomful tones,
echo ancient sounds of warning.
Street-crowd faces in public squares
await the terms of occupiers
and their too-familiar choice
of bullets or barbed wire,
whichever comes first.

Nothing to See Here

How quickly great nations
accept brutal habits,
sensing shock at the errors
and terrors inflicted by others,
gazing through or around
what happens at home
or is air-shipped elsewhere
without return address,
as though a light-switch flick
darkens our mirrors
to the one-way glass
of a line-up room,
where we see no one
but strangers as suspects.

LIVE, FROM THE
WATER'S EDGE

Gathering of the Waters

Tsunamis will wash away our other problems.
A tiny earthquake could launch the end,
dissolving threats of overflowing downhill brooks
choked with free-grown weeds turned trees.
As climate change and builders
race to see which inundates us first,
turns out neither match the soaring tide.
In the footage of tsunami wreckage
we sense high-water marks of fear.
The tsunami is our leading nightmare.
As bad dreams go, it tops the charts,
an island shrink might tell you,
as one of them explained
when I described my handcar
race against enclosing breakers
on Kalanianaole Highway,
a busy road we live near by the sea.
In sleeping fright emerging,
it's the kind of looming wave
that rains down somewhere else
until too late we learn it's also here.
Close calls and alarms
recur for dwellers of the zone.
The last one failed to hurl the waters
up to meet our hectic
early off-work, traffic-clogging
panic preparations.
Good news in disguise,
as the no-show flooding spared

an unintended motorcade,
pre-rush hour bumper-queued,
a cortege bypassed by disaster
on the real Kalani highway
of my frantic handcar dream.
Ocean elevating out of bounds
sweeping beyond its lapping borders.
roaring loose in streets and yards,
spreeing skyward all in its reach,
swallowing life and objects
that support the routine order
of weather vanes, traffic lights,
road signs, porches, steps and railings,
cars and trucks adrift without direction.
The neighbors' spreading monkey pod
may soon lurch upside down,
its roots, the strands of evolution,
tangled swirls in overruling ocean.
Awake, we'll drive to hilltop vantage,
watching, knowing lowland others
may be wading through their bedrooms,
treading current near a stranded mail box,
swimming at a roof-top level,
or clinging to rowboat life
in a measureless point-to-point
overturning disarray of limits,
as we once thought we knew them.
The phone book warning map
shows us tsunami's boundary edges
based on last year's water line,
as if the Pacific knew or cared
or got the CD memo saying where to stop.

34

Witness the rising sea's alert
and horror visions come to life.
When the nightmare turns real,
waking up will be too late
to greet the towering crash
of Hokusai's real waves
with sayonara or good-bye.

Of Islands and Outcomes

How did you wind up in Hawai'i?
A great circle's arc, a lunar eclipse,
coincident links of an undersea chain,
you also could say in a roundabout way.
A friend introduced him to a Senate clerk,
a girl from Maui he later married,
their first date free seats at a circus,
foreshadowed high-flying hand grasps
and long-term balancing acts.
The company he worked for bought
a paper in islands she came from.
As a mainland owner distrusted by locals,
it found a D.C. staffer with family out here,
who knew the players, to help ease the way.
Dots connected like undersea craters,
new man in charge with local in-laws,
well-placed island friends and others
in high places elsewhere
issuing Capitol sendoff cheers.
Big jobs don't always go to the skilled
but to those who flash a bright look
to readers and promise to holders of shares.
Lucky timing and opportunism,
grumbled some. It took *pull* to get in
and *push* to get out, to quote the signs
on the newsroom glass doors,
and their point about that was?
Merit doesn't win every call;
he'd seen that often enough.

His wire-balance act had
plenty of net to protect from slips.
Toehold achieved, occupation advanced,
but daily defending with missions
of search and annoy,
both chasing news
and hounding staff,
kept the tensions alive and on edge.
Lunar child's birthdays came and went,
objects in the sky easy to confuse—
his the satellite powered to ebb
seas and flow human moods,
but not the sun's growth control,
though it might on some days eclipse it—
like holiday fireworks disguised
as sparks of command
that burned and glowed,
bursts of direction not fully approved,
and maybe the cause of a firing next time.
After a decade in charge,
the top-floor comfort zone loomed,
but owners liked looks of new faces
with different roots from far-off places.
The look-good goals that set him up,
now worked to eclipse his own glow.
He lateraled well but missed the spot
he wanted above the cubicled terrain,
gaining instead deep furrows of effort
under new levels of pre-dawn sun.
Cross-fired, whipsawed with too much time
in grade and too little leverage left to resist,
he saw it was time to shut up and write.

Papers were sold, and sold again,
then sold once more in a swap
where the seller helped float the deal.
Action in a game of throw-ins
he watched from a place
where food, cars and homes
scrambled for dollars from space they bought
to pay for the papers' smart talk and buy-outs.
Two raised kids, a sea-world net gain
of loaves and fishes from bread-winning wife,
retired on Aina Haina's sacred ranch land,
planting avocados, watering ginger,
gathering coconuts, growing poems,
feeling some sense to it all in long runs
on a marathon course that sweetened
weekends like the relief of editorial endings
with the punch of a closing sentence.
Newspapers that were his life,
until they weren't,
now scrimp to pay their own bills,
cutting pages and bumping staff.
Having worked for them so long,
he reckons with their pain.
Reading six papers a day,
he pays to help keep them alive,
as they did him and his, in days,
nights and decades of week-to-week years,
of trapeze paycheck survival.

Waterfront of Many Dreams

Blurred reflections
waterscape our memories,
with colors that shimmer
in dreams recalling hidden towns
we know we've seen before
but can't remember where.

How often we find ourselves
riding downhill to the waterfronts
of busy streets (Dubuque or Newburgh;
Ohio River towns like Gallipolis;
or Providence, or the Anacostia in D.C.,
passing sites from distant days.)

What lurks in these hazy vistas
are shapes of places people work
and maybe live, roads where hauling,
shipping share a block to sip dawn coffee
or a day-ending beer close by
a brick-front home on a sidewalk's edge.

The gauzy view of silos gold and pink
surprising structure walls hint at fright,
driving down toward rivers of anxiety,
steering steeply from a third-deck wheel
above cobblestone road 40 feet below
on shaky tires against a river cross-wind.

Shining drab of a mirrored milling scene
lets unseen life continue in a setting
blinded to pursuits of wandering dreams.
Sleeping eyes pry open with relieving joy,
as waking moments clear the landing picture
of a troubled mystery, if not its whereabouts.

By a Stream of Consciousness

Tranquility wafts again past his sliding windows,
its breezes riffling coco palms, hanging ferns,
leaves of thirsty avocados,
and with it a current of rambling contentment,
mingling confusion about what in the day
seems to have mattered most.
Thoughts stray to creatures pausing to sip
at the springs to calm the heat of their hunger
and of mythical species that flew
with the spirit of fantasized faith.
How dreams imagine star-sprinkled unicorns
descending from clouds of enchantment,
while nature launches hungry jaws
stalking those born to be victims.

The quiet calm tempts his perusing
to the work of St. John of the Cross
about "Lions, harts, leaping does,"
including "Birds of swift wing,
mountains, valleys, banks, waters, breezes,
heats and terrors that keep watch by night..."
Comfort that may come from early texts
adjusts to what later may be read into them.
Scholars cannot agree how many
authors of scripture were the ones
who really did the writing.
Someone said or wrote these thoughts,
though *someone else*, we're told, recast them,
and yet the pollinated words arouse
wonders still in the rhythms of faith.

The older man regards the course of time
changing worlds of influencers,
flowing together like a bed of water,
Arthurian in its misty treasures.
In a quiet afternoon he recalls an aimless youth
propelling objects forward and retrieving them,
a bouncing ball on wooden steps,
a wound-up string spooling out and back,
recoiled actions of rote belief,
concentration for its own sake,
with a mission unspoken until
future hands translate the meanings
of contented silence.

A Bridge Too High

It was dark when I ran across the Mississippi
that September morning in St. Paul,
an early pre-dawn jog
before an '89 conference start.
I remember taking a slightly uphill right turn
with traffic and not clearly seeing
I was heading across the great divide.
Railings appeared to the right of me,
the sidewalk suddenly shrinking,
it seemed, to a narrow ledge;
lights in the distance and far below
flickering at infinity depth
on the face of the Father of Waters.
This jogger wearing bifocals saw it all
through a glass darkly—a St. Paul moment,
hopefully no fall from horseback
or anything higher than the fears
of a vertigo-saddled mind
that could only tell itself,
"Too late to turn back. You won't
like yourself if you do."
So much for the self-love of charity.
Time to shift into faith and hope
the other side was not the evil twin
of these two river cities.
On solid land after a third of a mile,
then a right turn downhill
to a riverfront park below,
where buses formed up,

43

to offer less daunting returns.
But no bus rides were ready just yet,
as the sun showed its waking signs.
Jogging back would make the river
more easily viewed in dizzying detail.
Conference breakfast beckoned,
a gathering of editorial wisdom,
critics with low regard for indecision,
in no mood for "on the other hand" options.
So back up and onto the bridge,
carefully watching two lanes
of oncoming Twin-Cities traffic,
one step at a time, not on the sidewalk
but using the gutter, looking only ahead,
anxious to see the nearing downtown
of welcoming St. Paul hotels.
At breakfast, a casual sightseeing mention
prompted my confident story of jogging
over the bridge, back and forth,
with been-there-done-that assurance,
my points made quickly and matter-of-fact,
as a pundit might do in advising Corinthians.

Remembered Reflections

Washing July sawdust from winter's ice,
cut and dragged from frozen lakes,
stored in summer sheds,
piled tightly as giant bricks.
Swinging picks and gripping tongs
launched glacial cakes to the tractor bed,
for pick-cutting to ice-box shapes;
hand-chipping blocks with sleetlike
spatters flaking guest-cabin floors,
to tailor each chunk and mop-dry the mess.

How much like our memory
that challenge takes shape:
cleaning, hauling, aiming for gem-setting fit,
cool in the craft as a diamond cutter,
but now recalling kitchens's wet clutter,
youth's untidy details of what really happened.
Memory shows neat-edged spacing
in opening flashes, but then gives way
to protrusions of jagged parts
too rough to slide into place.

Memory now betrays what we'd wished,
as mirrors of mind yield reflection.
And the point where certainties shift
grows harder to find, much like a line
somewhere in the water, where objects rise
from a seeming seam between similar
scenes reversed and remembered,

linked as twins in fading time,
old brethren players re-cast
in shimmered shadows uneven.

So much recalled from days
of blossom and hopes reaching upward,
petals and stems, hands and lips,
sudden breaths and murmuring
sounds beginning and ending with M,
mirrors, memories and eager eyes,
so long to live, so much to gain.
When did the bright dazzle dim
and cross the line of likeness
to images changing in place?

Did we let creatures of dread insinuate
in gardens we held but grew too late?
Was it memory's misgiving,
or real recollection,
that led to resetting past steps
on paths to measured revisits
for poems now fermented with doubt?
Think video replays of error,
instant but never-ending,
fresh flaws evolving with each review.

Recall seems to grow disillusion
on promised days and secret nights,
focusing episode faults
on things that went wrong.
Reveries that excited now lie
amid brown matted needles

at the feet of the pines
where young strangers
sat and talked; late afternoon
to morning lights on waters before them.

Reflective horizons of life emerge
from dawning seas and awaiting lakes.
What will you do with what you have learned?
Answers, vague then, echo more so today.
A pained re-gathering of awkward times,
shares visions of night moments in cars,
on steps, in doorways and halls;
springs on basepaths, harsh cinders in fall,
alone facing keys, at desk or in flight,
to make things finish, arrive at all-right.

The Waters of Memory

My brain keeps sending pool reports
on places we swam in summers past.
They frame the splashing fantasies
that rise to mind like measures
of fluid scaling thermometer tubes
in overflow temperature mode.

Do I trust this aging remote recall
on how I spent years of vacation months?
Like accepting second-hand details
of another reporter's eyes or ears,
from a scene where most are outside,
wondering if maybe memory is fiction.

Can these mental dispatches provide
the deep dive I want into the Hudson?
There, too steep a plunge at low tide
coated a slime-green goatee
on the face with squishy sludge toes
when standing to wave and grin.

Does my memory of muddy head-firsts
suffer from previous infantile limits,
a paralysis of knowing how it felt when
parents told us the waters we swam in
were too much like sewers and blamed
the army base offal for new crippling germs?

Some shared pools of rich friends,
basked as guests at estates, or joined the YMCA:
no trunks, no girls, never clear who was welcome there.
Others discovered a public pond whose waters
looked and felt like the olive drab Hudson
but was somehow okay to float in its broth.

Summers frame-flash in cinema blurbs.
Polio's scare hung about us,
a high-diving board, casting shadow on waters.
Friends in leg braces and voices grown weak
returned to remind us we swam
with viral agents of threatening times.

Our family swam in vacation lakes
with native names or at the ocean
in rented cabins by the shore of the Cape.
Five of us filled a Ford sedan, decades
prior to Interstate travel, when Route 1
and parkways were slow paths to the sea.

My pre-mortem revisits a dog-paddle
crossing of Little Sunapee and back,
days in pools at Tallman and Palisades Park
and a new one named for "Mad" Anthony Wayne,
teal rectangles of chlorine-spiked brine,
veining gold sparkles in glittering sun.

The parks we worked as attendants in summer
had bathroom stalls we cleaned at our peril.
Flushless waste splattered into chambers,

vaulted dark pools of suspended untreated,
manually drained and hose-cleaned,
scrub-broom disinfected each Monday.

Days after weekends meant dumping,
cleaning up after city dwellers
and Jerseyites, enjoying good times
in a park with a waterfront view,
had picnicked and played beside
stray copperheads and a poisoned river.

Wire-caged baskets filled
with our table clearings
tempted birds like standing buffets,
and any Sunday night rain,
doubled the weight of the lifting
onto fly-friendly trucks for collecting.

Summers of rivers, lakes, oceans, pools,
and the people stuff that went with them
challenge the memory to convey it all.
Yet, how much does it filter the flow?
The mind lingers in puddled reveries,
viewing days passed as waves to distant shores.

Another Neptune Production

The sea is a theater of its own wide casting
with many repertories of players to brighten
scene changes emerging in stages
from all directions of enter and exit
in colors and shapes and schools.

Costumed for underwater flight,
saucer-canopied Man-of-War hovers
in tasseled spacecraft design
drawn to chambered nautilus focus
above a moon-tinged ocean floor.

There, hybrid life plays
unexplained cameos, passing
through infinity's lensed diorama,
Moorish idols and tentacle squid,
nodules of coral, ribbons of kelp,
buried creatures springing forth,
to encounter performing rivals of prey
with appetite license to sample
bites of the scenery.

Unaccountably evolving mermaids
of undersea woodlands make their social debut,
centaured horned deer in ballgown bustles,
dancing across a proscenium
that spans the universe floor
in quick-changing acts without end.

Landmarks of Refuge

The song I hear when sensing the end
of a dream that took a wrong turn
is the 1919 runaway hit,
an anthem promoting out West
as the place to "find perfect peace"
from a world in royal flames
luring this side of the ocean
to douse them with blood
and Belgian-French mud
dug to rearrange lines
of old family thrones,
yielding sashes and swords
to embalm their powers
for Europe's fatal display.

So, the big escape song
of Ernest Ball and J. Keirn Brennan
outlived the war to end all
and others that followed
plus those who sought to avoid them,
and could be heard soaring
above campus barrooms
in rathskeller serenades
or at Sunday night sings
around parlor pianos,
its lyrics of lonely hope
a joyful wish forever after.

"With someone like you"
is how it proposed
to "a pal good and true,"
a faraway sheltered world,
"a sweet little nest
somewhere in the west,"
a retreat "across the great Divide"
to a land "known to God alone"
waiting "beneath a kindly sky."
Flatland prairies and mountains
beckoned as hideaways to nourish
ark-like feelings of species survival.

Ghost towns and mining sites
gave an early West its shabby,
dispirited look of long on empty,
but history renewed itself decades later,
staking outskirts in rendezvous chic
with Formica, tile and carpet;
Naugahyde, smooth and dark;
desert remote but neon cozy,
fueled by gas pumps shaded
under mustard pastel canopies.
Unleaded high-octane irony
lends bleaker meaning to the brand
of abandoned fuel tenant, Shell,
a label with a footnote echo
of igniting internal combustion,
in a handy place where folks met and drank,
escaping into motel arms across the lot.

Here was a site for wayside adventure
in sandy seclusion before the Interstate
planted the shield of its blue highway flag
near a cloverleaf on-ramp next town over,
signaling change to make the future
a thing of the past, like words in a song,
"let the rest of the world go by."

How Things Work

Sliding under a car to check what's wrong
is a dirty job best left to others,
an option that grows by the day
when it comes to all else we don't understand
or take the time to find out.
Machines and systems get it done,
as we pay the bill and wait for results.
Many can't find the handle to open our hoods,
much less look to see what's going on there.
At work, our devices lead secret lives:
pencil sharpeners, water coolers, staple guns.
Technicians on call thaw office computers
when screens freeze and keyboards turn cold,
rescuing copy machines when the paper won't feed.
Call the guy with the wrench who knows
color-code wires to save our DIY fix-its
from flying sparks and frying connections.
All around us experts are spreading,
pairing job skills with titles defying description—
systems analysts, facilitators,
influencers, coordinators,
diagnostic monitors, adjusters,
moderators, project counselors,
code interpreters, context framers, outcomes shapers—
and does a software engineer design lingerie?
The TV set, once an on-and-off thing
with a handful of channels,
has become its own world
in charge of our minds,

time and patience we can feel
streaming away as we work the remote,
the right word to describe our chances
of finding the movie we want
without signing up for a membership app
luring us in for seasons of binging addiction.
Or call the cable company for help,
which they can do when it comes to plugs
and rebooting but often will claim
nothing to do with the content we've bought
from platforms that make their own rules.
Moving away from things mechanical,
cargo-cult mystery systems have spoiled us
into acceptance—USPS brings us Amazon stuff;
the city hauls away rubbish, recycling.
backyard branches, and leaves;
one flush and away goes whatever
we no longer need to be with us;
a faucet turn washes our hands and brains
of having to think how all this happens.
And not to change the subject,
since maybe it doesn't,
how much else do we let slide
away and under concerns of a world
in which we give a headshake
and shopping-cart shrug
to a family berthed, marking time
in a tent on the sidewalk,
or those we don't see
locked from view in systems
even the experts can't fix.

Rainbows Are the Prize

Years ago when I came here
I said as a cynic might to a savvy friend,
"It's where the rainbow's end meets the bottom line."
A career move was the reason
with family income upgrading a lure,
to work for a media chain mining gold
from the minds of its readers,
selling space to those eager to tell what they sold,
whether stores or airlines or land on the market.
Rainbows have arched their spectral hopes
before these eyes for decades now,
colors clear even as once 20-20 views
passed through bi-focal phases.
Still forming above our valley,
they celebrate a concurrence
of sun and rain,
the curious yin-yang grasp
of joy and melancholy,
that clashing life drama
so strongly at play among in-laws
who grew up here heartened
by spontaneous colors,
knowing how soon they might fade.
Each sighting of overarched stripes
flashes thoughts of what I had quipped
in sardonic days past.
The fortunes so many had chased
came to pass for some over time,
outliving, one prays, the sell-by date

on a devil's deal that sold coming here
as a trade in titles to share a task master's mission
in a pot-of-gold era almost forgotten.
The rainbow endures as a sign
of hope in a place unconcerned
with its branding for causes,
sports teams or other group efforts
uniting people of caring and courage.
No one owns the rainbow:
it can't be sold fee-simple, rented for viewing
or leased to develop for off-shore investors.
Watching in wonder each time it arcs upward
and down suggests its end is its promise,
a treasure whose value is seeing the next one.

CRACKING THE
TIME-CAPSULE CODE

A Compass of the Mind

I look to the morning sun
through a childhood home window,
peering back through 70 years,
past where the rays came
through our crabapple branches
and the neighbor's cherry boughs,
shading his gray-shingled mansard roof
rising above the Hudson,
downhill, out of sight,
below the trees of our village horizon.

That was my East and remains
a mind's reference archived
in place behind my eyes' direction.

West was uphill to the school
where we ran each fall and trained
also to learn stop-and-start moves
with clutch and hand brake
to parallel park on a climbing grade.

North was the backyard, ours;
the talkative Renaissance neighbor's;
the confident shoe-store family of ten;
the village-line sign welcoming all
into Upper Nyack, home of a shipyard
and workers, a place of rough kids,
and millionaires with river views

their sloping lawns behind brick walls,
and the Hook, a mountain park
beside a hideaway girls summer camp.

South was Hart Place, a short street,
massive shady oak grown tall in its middle,
that angled from a T first left, then right,
past Edward Hopper's house
toward downtown's street-front stores
easily at home in his lonely paintings.

My upstairs southeast corner
window gave a desk side view
of that connecting link called Hart,
as an aging model Emerson
played Nashville songs from WPAT,
a Jersey station in Paterson-Passaic,
as I tried to write about minor
league ballplayers living
on $25 a week between bus trips
to small-town rooming houses.

I witnessed their post-war hopes
but did not live their dreams,
or mine of writing the bush-league book
that others since have done better.
But I did the neighborhood
rooming house thing
in places elsewhere,
a story for another day.

In searching for direction
I find the sun and think
in terms of bedroom windows,
fitting its morning fire into view,
sensing its afternoon glow
setting its crest on the hill.

In all this time, framed points
of a local mind still chase big-city aims,
writing of sharing ambition to grow,
nursing the hunger of waiting
to sounds of rural tunes lulling
a world of wallpapered hopes
and its someday yearnings.

My north star was the Hudson
though it remained east every day,
guiding my bearings around it
in a compass that still spins
a lasting sense of inner eye
back to a windowed room
with an eastern view
and music from somewhere out west.

Life Riverlasting

In those early war years we swam in the Hudson
until that summer '43 day
when mothers on shore
at Woods's Beach in Grand View
waved us in and then out with bad news
about the river and why its waters
could cripple our futures.
Early gossip blamed Camp Shanks,
the nearby staging base for troops
shipping off to fight in Europe,
but that fault faded as we figured
out what came from where
into the green-brown, olive-drab river,
three miles wide where we swam,
moving to and from our shores—
sludge from local factory dumpings
and flushings from our inner workings.

The dots at last had connected
like random pins on a campaign map,
and villages piping raw wastes
into the tides and currents
emerged as the cause of the poison
that could shrivel young arms in mid-reach
and paralyze legs from bending in motion.
What many knew had impaired the limbs
of FDR himself could also happen to us.
No more leaping from ten feet off the dock

at high tide on a family beach further north,
a level of bravery we inched our way toward
and finally gained the courage to jump.

The two-lane street we lived on
wound along the Hudson's western edge
and fit its name of River Road.
Land above it sloped into woods,
the West Shore railroad tracks
and beyond that, upper level places
we could see but never went to visit,
a missionary training school
and a convalescent home,
where pale-skinned bathers lived
and sometimes shared our river beaches—
refugees from Europe, we were told,
enjoying our amber waves of polluted freedom.

Wars and decades later, treating
of sewage and wastewater filters
made Hudson swimming technically safe,
but people seemed to distrust the numbers
claiming polio'd really been beaten,
as pools, clubs, lakeside and ocean resorts
grew comforts outshining the lure of the river.

Those who once swam in its waters
have turned their time in the Hudson
into boasts of adventure, bodies sheathed
by exposure to world-beating germs,
bred in the cauldrons and guts of conflict,

hoping our cure by immersion
outlasts the hidden due date
of its unwritten barcodes.

Recurring Flavor

Candy canes survive
as holiday symbols
of our ambivalent ways,
"delicious ambiguities" to some,
sugared devices to guide the disabled,
the old returning each year to celebrate,
objects whose mint taste never changes,
though purposes flash in and out of meanings,
giving support to traditions
in serious shepherd-staff scenes,
then jumping to jolly rhythms
as something a tap dancer'd use
to lean on while clicking the shoes,
stabilizing images that balance feelings
of holy sharing with self-adoring hope,
joy reserved in part for family friends
with kettle-drop deductions
for distant strangers.

The color scheme lends itself
to uniforms of young hospital helpers,
a curious flag-patterned mix
of bloodshed, bedsheets and soap,
sanguine purity chasing errands of health.

To winter skating with my father
I took the bamboo cane we kept at home,
a souvenir from somewhere warmer,
and as a child thought it was funny

to hook the handle through blades of his moving skates.
The Dad connection sadly worked,
but his own accountant's sense of balance
saved him from falling, striking back,
or ever raising the issue or object again,
perhaps a secret early-life awareness
of the Cain and Abel streaks in all of us.
Disturbing memories keep that ice pond
scene alive, his wildly flailing dance to stay afoot,
a frozen haunting, peppermint reminder
of a father's forgiving patience,
and the good-and-evil intertwine
I worked a lifetime to contain,
like swirling stripes of contradiction
locked in seasons of truce.

Hats of Fantasy

I grew up in a world of Fedoras,
the hats men wore to show who they were,
though Sarah Bernhardt wore the first one
in an 1883 French play titled *Fedora* she starred
in as a countess with the first name, Fedora.
It must have been a good look that led
men to grab it as a crown of their own.

My father's, a dark gray-green felt,
fit me fine. I wore it to church on Sundays,
even after a rich friend scolded its shape
and a growing hole in the front of its crown
worn by thumb and forefinger removal
over too many years of indoors and out,
between tree-rack at work and coat hook at home.

I was not alone in wearing such hats;
Mondays after Easter, grade school boys
in the factory town I went to by bus
dressed Sunday best with long pants,
jackets, ties and Fedoras to the brim
of adult simulation, acts of faith in fashion
by parents possibly trying the future
on for size, modeling men who worked
in the city, and not at box-making
in the cardboard plant on the pier.

Fedoras were my hats of fantasy
worn by detectives working a search
or crooks on a job in the dark.
When I saw five men in a roadster
all with Fedoras and suits, bunched together,
their profile as gangsters en route to a crime
flashed on my brain like a WANTED sign.
From there private eyes took over my script,
hard-boiled Dick Powell, Tom Conway's *The Falcon,*
Humphrey Bogart, Dana Andrews, Chester Morris
as *Boston Blackie,* Lloyd Nolan as *Martin Kane,*
and who bore his lid with more edge than *Dick Tracy*?

These parts preempted a pre-teen phase
of a kid who later would view a missed life
of roles he might have been cast to play.

Some days I wore the hat to the movies
and carried a hard plastic gun in my pocket,
a semi-convincing toy in the shape of a small .45.
It was all an act, but who knew?,
as I took back streets to reach home
after slipping out a theater side door.
My private-eye world skirted the classroom
where hard rules banned objects of threat
and the comic books promoting their use.

The radio *True Detective* phase passed,
most of my mysteries unsolved,
but the hat fixation held fast,
even as wearing them eased out of style
with the fading of Danbury's place at the top,

when a stylish president declined
the gift of their hats. In sad hindsight,
the hatters should have built one
for Texas motorcade safety.

No longer the head dress of youth, Fedoras
survived on heads of FBI sleuths,
NFL coaches, braided men of strong faith
and cigar-smoking moms of the Andes.
Period movies of yesterday's shadows,
film noir agents of war and depression,
make great reminders today
of how grown men looked
and little boys tried to.

Time Alone

Welcome to the hermit culture,
reclusive in its crablike charm,
secretly appealing to an aging moonchild
once relieved by limited options
of rainy Saturdays canceling
yard-work duties, allowing
radio morning escapes
to adventures of others.

Life alone has gone viral
and virtual coping seems to return
self-absorbed youth to its old-age version
of electric travel, linking
Let's Pretend to Grand Central Station,
"crossroads of a million lives" then,
to faces Zoomed alive elsewhere now
on our checker-squared gallery screens.

We can now interact in compartments
with options to shift to the face you want
and silence your mic to make clear
you listen mostly in therapeutic cutoff,
absolving the noncommittal from guilt
of withdrawal, a press box of sorts
for the socio neutral, observing
the radio silence of remembered youth.

Flash back to the quieted Swiss,
resting their multilingual
echoes in lakefront serenity
that may seem like surrender
but could be a white-cross strength
that calmly awaits understanding.
Isolation frees up tasks dictated
more often by habit than need.

Spare time should return to memory's
general fund for re-use in reclaiming
preferred past days, to share with strangers
in a break from meeting-fatigue,
giving many a rest from each other
in the masked guise of health and safety,
a respite from drives to save humanity,
a pit stop on caring's long road to curing.

Overcast

Sunday afternoon in gray September,
home to early clouds of ocean north and east,
its bay a mile or so from the piano
where you played *Autumn Leaves*,
each slicing note sounding off the walls
of an art gallery, open somehow
to the four of us dating under its dome.
Kosma's cosmic notes seemed tuned to trees
on the campus and neighbor streets,
a sadness too soon for 20-year olds
weaving their weekend letdowns
with overthought plans for what next,
scored and scripted for branches of sorrow,
destined in later decades to be real,
a future unfurling in dismal ribbons.
Your music that day was not the jazz,
the double-quartet, or the off-key beer,
with all its table-pounding cheer
of the night before's tweed skirts
and studied cigarette wavings,
joining boys in sweaters and flannels,
'50s students with '20s envy,
white bucks and buttoned-down blue,
a fashion salute to yesteryear's dreams
feeling our way toward fantasy comforts.
You spoke of your life among others,
of young men and their actions,
as though you saw with the eyes
of Edith Piaf or Marlene Dietrich's

lamplit view with a Barbara Stanwyck vibe,
shrugging time lost in courting styles
when the canals of Venice awaited
the prodding of gondoliers' oars,
that you nailed in a moment from nowhere,
breaking into the *Barcarolle*
out of the gray, amazing us all
as your hands moved over the keys,
playing Offenbach's classic
there in the vacant hall
with other works of the past,
unaware in our premature thoughts
these were moments of promise
we'd live to disappoint.

Entangled Bliss

How quickly the placement of features
draws our gaze to the face of attraction:
the look of the eye, curve of the nose,
full bow of lips, capture our view
and hold us hostage to first impression.
Only later does our vision recognize
the looping, lurking inner edges
beneath what makes the pattern
of the profile thrive in our longing.

How awareness of loose ends grows
with fragments and haphazard circuits
linking coexistent objects obtruding
in their process of random suspension,
overlapping in a jagged melange
of misfit and function to convey
a chronic rendition of disarray,
and illustrate terms we soon see as part
of commitment's sealed bargain.

How the bill of particulars builds
among the phobic shadows casting
depression, confession, moods of distress,
as we witness moments of ailing
alone in waiting-room *tableaux*,
missing hours of unexplained time,
surfacing traits of trouble signs,
arrows pointing to breakdown lanes.

How the symmetrical sweetness that drew us
into the deal of a lifetime continues its pull,
reminding us why we navigate deeper
daily kaleidoscope tests of faith.
Family riddles inhibit the quests,
extending them into decades,
clues within scope of plain sight
luring our focus to faint beams of origin,
guiding us through each new demand
of inherited chaos.

How we steer the craft
of understanding in patient hope
a some-day plan with gauging points
could make this uncharted travel
worth the face that lured us
into its mysteries.

Of Home and Hope

Parents-to-be, we moved
to a place where kids were allowed,
as incomplete as that spring
of expectant living.
Rug-coated stairway upstairs
to a two-room bungalow flat
on a street with few trees
but many fenced alleys
linked to more neighborhoods like it
on Columbus, Ohio's, plainer north side.
Downstairs, another part of a once one-family home
sheltered a couple from Cadiz, a coal-mining town
to the east, who whooped with friends
they invited for Saturday afternoon
watchings of TV pro wrestling,
blinds shut against distracting outdoors.

Upstairs we found fully-spread carpet
abundantly furled to the walls
and then under, blocking winter draft,
covering sockets, hiding other life.
Rolled back by us, it showed wood floors
beneath did not join those walls,
apart by a gap of inches enough
to unsettle recent-weds in their 20s,
awaiting arrival of life
dependent on them
for each moment of air
in a place where used rugs,

old chairs and dark sofas defined
their cradle of discontent
in an era when time
seemed bound in memory lock.

How did young easterners, we, move into
this hastily-cornered world standing still?
Escaping with 1960's black-and-white *Route 66,*
a TV *On-the-Road* refuge from settings like ours
where millions apparently lived,
as "pleasant peasants" in vicarious mode,
where Silliphant's Todd and Buz,
after Kerouac's Sal and Dean,
themselves sought ways out
from sinister smallness of middle borders,
lands of hopes quilted in mid-century
notions of freedom sewn tight
in designs of the past
and patterns of sameness.

No home for a newborn, we said,
as we covered the gray-brown
darkness afoot with a sheet
of a shiny "-oleum" flooring,
scrubbing and mopping to reach
mint sheen and hospital glow.
On it we based a second-hand crib
from trusted friends we knew
wouldn't brush its rails with poison
paint that might tempt infant gums.

That August day we brought baby home
from University Hospital
in our '53 Plymouth, brown,
and carried her upstairs,
we were cast as protectors
of fragile beings, including ourselves,
in an upstairs home as bad a fit
as its unfinished floor, stop-gap carpets
and lone stairway to enter and leave.

Two weeks later, mother and child,
(tiny survivor of Labor Day weekend
when drug stores were closed
with meds to slow runny innards
nowhere at hand, until boiled rice water,
bananas and tea stopped the flow),
left on a plane for New York,
met there and viewed by grandparents,
returned to Ohio, with child destined for travel,
next time a Plymouth drive of 600 miles,
a baptismal trip to Chicopee, Mass.,
warming a bottle at a home-based
gas stop in West-*by God*-Virginia,
thanks to the lady with kitchen stove,
someone we wouldn't have found on the Interstate,
fast roads still in the planning for years to come.

Then back from NY to Ohio by Plymouth
and east again within weeks to look for a job.
Providence at last! Returning westward again,
six states in one day, to bid Ohio goodbye.
Mom and baby flying East one final time,

young father, 25, driving a U-Haul attached,
a caboose of stuff from stop-and-start lives,
(emptying cargo to fix a flat tire at the start)
then engine revived by a random Triple-A truck
of Keystone roadside coincident luck
on Pennsylvania's edge-to-edge turnpike,
making it somehow to NY, CT and Rhode Island,
election night 1960, celebrating our own
New Frontier version of sorts.
Time for a launch of new work and fresh life,
where a child of 10 weeks re-started
her 60-year journey of caring
from a state flying "Hope" as its motto.

Places of Fiction, Faces of Truth

A daytime daddy with a nighttime job
read while baby napped; Mom worked,
or some days before leaving, she'd
let their little girl, nearly two, toddle
about the rental they were redoing
before leaving for work in her car.

In a TV world still black and white
covers of novels brought color to stories
still missing from gray screens at home.
Books seemed to pre-destine his path,
from *The Fires of Spring* and *Some Came Running*
to *Lolita* and *Goodbye, Columbus,*
topics and titles led through halls of mirrors,
delayed, distorted and blurring reflection
with hopes of the telling of fortunes.

A Walk on the Wild Side and *The Moviegoer,*
separate tales of the same swampy city
of lasting intrigue, flashed before him
comparable sides of divided worlds
he sensed in his own antique harbor
where words in print seemed the only escape.
As *On the Road* and *Of Time and the River*
detoured him to *Life on the Mississippi,*
The Deer Park extension of *The Day of the Locust*
lit the Hollywood world he dreamed
of approaching, Smith-Corona in hand,
to reach his next level of wonder.

The Winter of Our Discontent intruded,
a Steinbeck tale too close to home by cold chance
in an out-of-place venue of bad faith for some
and wrong-place, wrong-time mistrust for others.
After *Rabbit, Run* grated his conscience,
he shifted his Golden State viewer to north,
finding *A New Life* in fabled "Cascadia,"
Malamud's green northwest haven,
a Pacific state that seemed just right
as a refuge site for a family shadowed
by short-range horizons of Atlantic limits.

Baby became his daytime companion for errands,
hours of dream-reading, and later the typing
of letters to look for work elsewhere.

One day he awoke to the face of a child
dripping with paint—a can of light beige left open,
a still-life with roller, tray and an unfinished wall.
What followed saved the day for a paint-tasting
(water-based) child now 62 and a parent herself.
But the mix of sleeping, babies and books
remains a point in his past where dreams
of fiction leapt from their pages
to arrive at awakening truth.

The Journey Back

Something about the designer swirl
and the nest-spun strokes
of her done-up hair
told him the future of joy
was turning its back
on him and their life,
heading out and away
that night from this moment
of work and family together.

Someday the backstory of how
it all happened, how the signals
reached him in vertebral pattern,
blips flashing on a rung-step course,
would lend a symmetrical lustre
to tales of disclosed betrayal,
and then his recovery,
life going forward
from naked setbacks,
dodging snide taunts
and coiffed rebound gestures
to seek a beckoning freshness.

Now with enticements under control,
structured against disappointment,
bypassing risks of unsecured dreams,
he pursued life's frontal realities,
advancing, accepting the upswept glamor
of later success in stride with others

who'd made their marks younger,
yet still groomed their envy
to recall his rejection.

Back now to regain the forsaken,
he gauged safe travel to link
love's classic standpoints,
as though they were bones
of a body transformed
to junctions of life and career
in bittersweet glory,
pivot points displayed
to spread flanks and clasp
for dear life, as crossroads
encircled on a new map.

Many Trains of Thought

Hanging out on a train
is a writer's cozy adventure,
watching the windows of scenes
pass like story board moments
quick shots of life that seem to take shape
after they've passed
and tracked their way back
through the mind like some kind
of re-screening tunnel that cuts
out slow parts of the plot
you're directing yourself to script.

You think of Thomas Wolfe riding alone
in trains up the shores of the Hudson,
imagining lives of those he's spied
from a speeding anonymous distance.

Trains home at night from reporting in Boston,
witnessing warmly-lit windows
of flashing-by homes of families
with jobs who only worked daytime.
Trains from Providence to New York and D.C.
in search of new jobs in the '60s.
A '74 train from D.C. to a strange PA town
called Media, a curious place,
but fittingly named, to look for a writing job,
and start a poem on the trip home
of Queen Anne's lace growing wild
among hard lines of rails, ties and cinders.

The '86 trains we rode through the High ground
of Scotland, dour and rainy in wintry April,
gave us watery window lenses
to sense turning points in our world
of work in the sunny Pacific.
On a Delaware train to New York
two decades later, scribbling miles
of window sights in a notebook,
giant spools of thick cable, stacks of pipe,
sheds of cinder block, corrugated roof rust,
empty trucks and piles of tires,
frames and disjointed links
of equipment scattered in yards
near warehouse buildings,
nondescript workings awaiting
the next industrial call-up
to spring into use, unaware
it might replace them with buttons
and codes on a palm-sized screen.

How dramatic the '07 train
from Prague to Vienna,
border guards entering
our sliding-door compartments,
asking for our papers, and again
the same thrill of intrigue
from Vienna to Budapest,
a Hungarian rhapsody waiting
for uniformed guards
to sing questions, asking
about our mission on their soil.
Rail stops in Hapsburg-Iron Curtain fantasyland

went smoothly, and we've saved the photo
of the traveling writer as actor
in dark sweater and jacket
sipping from his cup of suspicion
in the club car, conveying the look
that combines wary and weary
in a straightforward glance
of well-traveled eyes masking
a storehouse of Cold War secrets.

Hanging out on a train can suffer down moments.
Once on the Amtrak Metro back to New York from D.C.
the engine broke down somewhere deep in New Jersey,
an unlit stretch of tracks next to nowhere.
A new locomotive coming to fetch us
took hours as we sat unmoving in limbo,
a tired writer feeling out of story ideas.

A Nation's Birthdays

Born on the Fourth of July was I,
a birthmark that's lasted a lifetime
of firecracker wisecracks,
songs by George M.
and many Cohan imitations,
Yankee Doodle babies, streaks of independence,
patriot dreams and moments of nightmare,
all shared with the rest of a nation
often in need of something to cheer.

What my parents were thinking that autumn
night in 1934 when their internal fireworks
led to launching a kid will remain
a Depression-era mystery,
1935 producing fewer births
than any year in that century.
The movie hit that year, *It Happened One Night*,
the top tune Benny Goodman's *Moonglow*.
Just right for a moonchild true to most Zodiac traits:
homebound, crablike, reclusive and cautious.
Depression infant, World War child, Cold War
service in peace as an Army lieutenant,
too old and too married for hazards that followed.
In 1985, lucky to have turned 50 in the 50th state,
celebrated with a too-clever column to say so,
funny and thoughtful to some,
pretentious self-preening to others.

The conflict of independence continues—
stay under your crab shell, behave
or burst forth in sparks of opinion,
kindling attention and drawing its fire.
Newspaper struggles grew islands of tension,
awash in currents of argued matters,
petty, major, vast and obscure.
Still celebrating one of many,
making a birthday holiday—
this one for Martin Luther King Jr.
What seemed a natural for the most diverse state
did not happen until 39 others chose
to make it a day-off in theirs.
Editorials and supporters' columns
overcame snide heckling
—another day off for state workers,
fears of commercial abuse,
lack of political interest,
top-floor questions
from nouveau skeptics
—and helped make it law in '88.

Some birthdays matter more than others,
as our nation flies stripes of alternate colors
beside its corner of stars, white on blue,
changing perhaps in some future day's flag
to a field of stars more like the faces and hands
of the millions who've given it life.

CONNECTING THE CURATED DOTS:

SOME ASSEMBLY REQUIRED

Closing Questions

When a golden era passes,
we hope we'll know the signs
in time to make our moves.
A creature in flight but off balance
considers the severed wickets
of exhausted piping
linking a future and past,
both seeming alike
in fadings of brilliance
at the glories of dusk.
Can an age promise more
than horizons continue?
The glow of saffron we worship
may already by fuming toward sulfur,
clouding a scene set for growth
with the haze of shortfall
and melting ambition.

How do we sense the fadeout
of time as we've lived it?
More of an oily smog
than bright-edged pages
of history's long print
stacked in hidden ingots
of leadership words
and celebrity wisdom.

Does an era reveal itself
with hints of dying glory?
As in that 1915 whiff of gas
in the toxic trenches of Ypres,
wafting a new awareness of death,
not a post-Edwardian exit,
disciplined heels in braided splendor,
but a breathless new start
in human reduction,
—industrial-strength,
mechanized impact—
losses loading ossuaries
with SRO remains to be seen.

Or how the champagne waterfall
splashed to an end at market bottom
before tuxedoed tipplers
figured out they were due at work,
lined up to find there was none.
As sentiment serenaded *steampunk*,
jazz and gin lit lyric ways to escape,
but the romance of wealth tripped
in guiding with guttered flames
and crashed to the sidewalks below.

We scan the fading colors
and wonder if we missed the turn
to the slow or sudden closing
felt in real time or seen rear view.
Were our pivots line-drawn
as we made then, or framed
for another day's capsules and shrines?

Nexus of Now and What's Next

Lines are plotting our lives
before we know what they mean
and why they criss and cross,
in a symmetry of faith,
connect and intersect,
shoot their azimuths
with seeming abandon,
creating networks of family trees,
blood lines indeed,
from which emerge
the shapes of treasure,
taking dimension and edging
toward our perceiving.
We with corners and angles
seem harnessed and linked to cell towers.
Unfathomed formations define
values in terms of directions,
bewildering wires and spokes,
expanding beyond us in patterns,
extending geometry's codes
that translate our measures of gauge
and space to ordered design,
saving the secret parts for readers
of nature between the lines.
Webs engage the nexus joints
in linear weavings of force and object,
thrust and traction, power and moment.
Underpinned by circuits of framing,
hints in astrolabe sightings,

strands of architect dreams,
lines and points excite us in ways
pilots and spiders can understand.

Mushrooms Emerge

Let us have pillows to match
our Technicolor dreaming!
Their cases once pending
from the courtyard clothesline,
drape now like flags awaiting salutes
from pageants that pass in review.
Top secret, we were told over sipping
beers in Ohio—experiments in mushrooms
were producing and directing
studies into button fungi
gathered from Mexico's caves
and smuggled hush-hush
to our then Columbian shores
for testing, sampling, launching
like a nighttime NASA project,
streaking somewhere dark and quiet,
floating sideways in a dreamy stare.
Who knew what they grew at OH-ess-yew,
let alone, more mysterious, why?
Many swore secrecy in that '60 scene.
Those who stumbled on it wondered
what's coming up here in Big Ten pastures
where experiments favored feeding
livestock's ground-game values?
Meanwhile, the psychedelic truffle
had flowered on its Ivy cusp
sprouting among green minds
in Dr. Leary's Harvard yard.
What color were our dreams

before the laboratory nibblings?
Too few had noticed to describe,
but soon the vivid splashes
seemed sacred swatches
from south of the border
for sewing the coat of Joseph,
a play that came years later.
Researchers whispered from
their psilocybin silos about
kaleidoscopic vivid visions,
shifting but still unshared,
outshining the spectrum
with color bursts beyond the rainbows
our unexpanded minds
too often settled to accept
against the choice of brighter options.
Something seemingly illegal
foamed above our malty speculation,
thinking color-coded pillow sheets
as the semaphore of progress
in the sheepskin world of secret linens.
But today, the need for cloak
and dagger's hidden 'shrooming
has yielded to publicity,
as scholars rush displays on screens
of research-grant achievement.
Journals, tomes and seminars
widely advertise on-line the work
no longer done in shadows by the CIA
on unsuspecting Free State inmates.
No longer needing the dark to grow,
mushrooms have risen unclouded

above the fears of social fallout,
skyward dreaming on a clean horizon,
swept clear by the brooms of science,
clandestine bedwear of the visionary past
now displayed in flying colors.

What Today Grows Tomorrow Leaves

How quickly it all can change,
seconds sprouting to moments
that stalk the wonder of life
in heart-cleft seeded leafings
from wisdom's tongue of potential,
flattering forth in the wit of ideas,
only to fall and curl with its age,
drying in forfeited growth.
What left the hearts of our mouths,
bright and apt for another time,
fades now in the dryness of leaves,
canceled as flawed and misgrown.

Disappointed, we persist
in a zest of outreaching stems,
our avocado souls opening lips
to rays of sunlight attending,
wooed by window-sill warming,
supine for bedding in lava soil.
Will this be the beauty whose branches
spread shelter of promise,
shades of evergreen hope?
Angelic eavesdroppers view,
helpless to garden our season of coaxing,
but praying we get some of it right.

Bank Shot

Escheat is the noise
the sneakers make
on the floor of a court
when the game is afoot
in pursuit of a ball,
passed, bounced, aimed
toward a net result.
Banks use the term
as one of default,
a ball bouncing freely
with no one to claim it,
a feudal tab regarding
unclaimed assets
yielding to forfeit,
and a label these days
for lack of action.
Depositors seek the rim
and knotted strings attached,
rushing before closing buzzers
to angle a hopeful carom
at a suspense of hanging threads.
In chasing rebounds,
of moneyed indecision,
the shortest route may be
a ricochet off the boards.

Blue Bowls Await Discovery

It's all about the blue bowl,
an object never out of place.
How many cradle plants in porch and yard?
Blue bowls serve with unappreciated value
though their presence may span the ages.

A vessel cracked from time-travel shipping
rests at the scene of suggested ruins,
empty but soon to be used by a mythic
beauty checking her wrist
as if for the time or water heat.

Blue bowls sent quiet signals of grace
long before the birth of satellite dishes,
containers here to be noticed and filled
and possibly one day to be heard,
reservoirs of sound awaiting human code.

A museum bowl we admire looks
to have arrived at the wrong address,
an unworthy site in ruined history,
but as a basin of serene use,
it remains to give shape to its contents.

Omar Khayam saw heaven in its image:
"that inverted bowl we call the sky."
Alice Walker saw in "My Mother's Blue Bowl"
a family's enduring kitchen artifact
of patience to nourish survival.

Flights of Fancy

The courting gesture spreads its wings
for an airborne approach
to splash land with likely action
of a brisk and feathery sort
in the shallow waters.

Note how the angled legs
and spiky feathers
gear outwards to sustain
a fluttery brash encounter,
reminiscent of Zeus'
swanlike approach to Leda
and all that unfolded
from that hybrid animation.

But the calm she-bird wading,
and perhaps waiting, in shallow surf
may, or may not, be asking:
is this a social visit, or
are that guy's wing tips
as grabby as they look?

This outreach moment
could extend avian
family life of the wetlands
in a righteous passage of nature.
So different from advanced-life love
where formal alerts now seem preferred
for the grounded steps of mating creatures:

are you flirting with me?
like old declarations of war
now required to engage in life.

No more beachhead landings
for romantic incursions
by the office cooler
or copy machine,
where only the bubbles rise,
and reproducing's a paper act.

Fashion Fits the Moment

No one seems overdressed
for the big reveals that unfold
in parting mist, unclouding surprise.
As we wait to see the approaching face,
we may miss the embered glow
of a burning tree, lost, it seems,
in the hand-held folds of a matching gown.

Distracted, we double-take later,
recalling the flame-tinged alarms
of enraptured signs before us,
or perhaps in rear-view departure.
How captivating this emergence looms
through haze of windshield or mirror
in the role of a roadside reminder.

The man, jut-chinned at the ballroom table,
smiles in his starch-collared tux at us
and each award-waving speaker.
We see him and his admiring lady
friend's insistence that black tie and pearls
would be more required than optional
at this dinner for the feeding of trophies.

The brunette in the hotel lobby,
in her blue bare-shouldered gown,
waits alone for a cab to deliver
her in a fish-tail-length dance dress
to the Gayety Theater a few blocks away

on historic East Baltimore Street,
where the gown zips off near the foot lights,
timed with offstage music behind,
sudden details against a dark curtain,
a dissemblage of nets, hooks and eyes
tying fashion-fed views to witnessing gazes.

The evening wear of an Army guest captain
seemed more for an usher or bellhop,
tight waist-length jacket with big epaulets,
pillbox hat with '50s chin strap,
though this right dress might be simpler
for fighting men to explain
than each desert clash of prophetic flames.

Appearances can serve rare purpose
when we learn ways they link our needs.
Every mission changes shape and color,
as the shifting cloth of seasons resurrects
feelings refitted in new shrouds of promise.

Curtains Set Sail

The see-through drapes behind me
give my Zoom-mates a window view
of Hawai'i, as I witness them or read
aloud of my own late visions of life,
from my sunny afternoon screen to their
night-time eyes and mainland ears.
Through the gauzy backdrop
they can see the ti leaves brush
in the breeze against our sliding panes.

Plumeria branches and the neighbor's house
obscure the ridgeline vista and its sprawl,
a spreading downhill sweep of sun-tiled
castle plazas sloping seaward,
to the gated entry-exit checkpoint booth
that guards its layered majesties.
Limply transparent, my drapes
only partly display what's at large
in our hidden Pacific afternoons.

What do they conceal or reveal
about the front-lit face of the poet
reading aloud from his papered disarray?
Windblown in storm, like sails burst free
from their ties, kinetic hanging shrouds
propel the moving sounds of reaching words.
Others elsewhere hear me shout into my screen,
wondering maybe, *What's he trying to tell us?*
or possibly, Where's he trying to steer us?

The fabric flutters loose to ride the traveling air,
coasting forth on pressured thoughts
billowing out in cheering gestures,
or perhaps as a gusting signal
of climaxing curtains soon to descend,
a coming down on closing words
from this screedy island performer.
Distant magic shifts both windows and screens
with a parting of drapes for new voices.

Straight up, or on the Rocks?

The free spirit lurks and considers
the hop to a fragile lookout
when planning its next move ahead.
Is what holds in place
this free-standing rock pile
glue enough to secure
the next leap to perch?
And what foundation
has been lumped together
by unfastened stones
resting in this configured
surface-to-surface design?
Alluring as they may be
to the flying shadow in waiting,
they suggest a trap,
a toppling boulder collapse,
on the wary pretender.
A short-lived top of the heap
haunts a cautious survivor
arising within the older campaigner,
chilled by memory's accrual
of past missteps adjoined
in happenstance cobblings
of contoured fittings that asked:
"What could go wrong?"
The wiser free spirit so far
has withstood the uneven risks
of "Up, up and away,"
a rally cry for prominence,

hesitation seeming the better part
of proudly mounting,
in ascendant display,
a platform held mostly by faith
in a treacherous balance.

Depths of Disclosure

Stare through the bottom of things
and feel the spiral pattern
of winding lines draw the mind
in hypnotic swirl to its starting point.
Consider the solar paths in place
before planets fell into orbit
on predestined lanes of travel.
Living lines assume dimension
and leap from memory to link
winding paths of life awaiting
fragments of episodes floating
in coils of reflection,
the pivot points that dot
the roundabout routes we follow,
blinded by the gyre next time.
As other seers have noted,
the deeper the gaze,
the plainer we notice
the swirling new lines
reversing the flow,
coming back to us,
blue from the dusty gold,
water up from the desert.
Faith pans for the future
in the dust of the past.
The crust of what we believe
we see has given way
in a puzzled approach
to our realm of origins.

Viewing a recoil of lines
reminds us we're sensing
an end to what little is left
that we thought might circle forever,
like the whorls in our prints,
confirming our presence and guiding
our hands-on probe into light years of soil.
At center we find a blank look
that questions: why are you here,
and were you surprised
staring deep in the Earth
could yield hard answers from heaven?

Short-term Serenity

Serenity's now an incremental thing,
no longer a long-playing epic
scored by allies of angels on Earth.
It's available now in cameo doses of sparkle,
followed by work-stops scheduled to calm,
emerging as makeshift plateaus in the hectic mind,
as the end of a hard task beckons
toward a programmed moment
of rest and reflection—but not too long.

Envision a series of stress-break dividers
planned to separate infinite deadlines,
queueing up in your tickler files
or hovering in space for landing instructions.

Memory spotlights days when life felt at ease:
deposits to rescue threadbare accounts,
brunch with a son after marathon finish,
the last week in April when taxes are mailed,
long special sections gestating for months,
done and delivered on newspaper doorsteps,
a swollen mind shrinking in postnatal haze
walking in empty-bliss mode nearly 12 miles home.

Serenity sneaks up in later life,
blooming in sprouts of contentment,
hard to explain without user guides.
Home late at night, I wheel green-waste carts
to the curb for collection tomorrow,

eyeing again the dark cosmic plenty
of distant light seedings and moon.
They are still there. I am still here,
surviving last week's life of the yard
and another night's planting of stars.

OTHER CREATURES, OTHER LIVES

A Reflection of Ducks

You were the little girl
intently handing corn
to the creatures at the edge
of the pond near your shiny shoes,
being careful of mud.
Your gray bonnet framing
sunlit curls gently shadowed
the top of your face,
leaving the rest bright
to look nearly angelic
above the dark collar
of your matching gray coat.
The photo I took of you
that day at Slater Park,
using the gray-green
squint-and-click
drugstore camera, somehow
caught the morning sun,
its companion shade
and the eager ducks
by the sequined waters
in a trademarked way
easily used in commercial joy,
a pastoral postcard
to persuade with image
of happy innocence in a place
by a pond at a zoo in Pawtucket.
Photo by dad of a child
still too young for school
but aware perhaps of parental drift.

Another young girl with ducks
is made of bronze and cheers
in playful breezy-dress pose
on the bandstand pond
at Oahu's Kapiolani Park
5,000 miles and 50 years later,
as waterfowl cruise by her statue
and beneath the sidewalk bridge
that arcs the waters winding though the park..
Runners relaxing from distance efforts
notice and maybe scatter
crusts and crumbs for the birds,
sharing the happy abandon
of the sculpted child,
as they greet fellow finishers
of the day's long course,
thinking of Sunday breakfast
or week-night dinners waiting.

The photo of toddler daughter
took on new growth at 8 x 10,
copied prints in holiday mails
reaching grateful families
who, unlike attentive ducks,
did not stay put, swim or fly
for long in domestic patterns.
Ducks seem kind examples
of reflective lasting joy,
but our visions of them
could be snapshots too,
of mallards or Hawai'i cousins
poised for a calendar photo,

framed as floating, placid
feathers that belie anxieties
on hold but soon to follow.

Feeding faith from caring hands,
spreading seeds and puff-popped kernels
from your hand-held cornucopia,
our '60s child in gray bonnet delivered
for years to your flocks at worship.

We too are migrants of fleeting fate,
Ohio daughter to New England, Palos Verdes,
Manhattan Beach and Santa Cruz,
flying back to her own family years
in Lake Bluff and Ingleside,
the horse-shoeing, home-roofing days,
the commute to Dubuque to earn your collar,
running the underdog Methodist
church in Jo Daviess' Stockton;
racing-car driver husband, two kids
there to pray with you Sundays;
the parish years in Wisconsin—
Cambridge, Burlington, Madison,
the West Allis amen finale,
then out on your own
with little kids grown,
race driver alone,
and late second husband
asleep under stone.

Unlike other seniors
seeking serenity's seasons in warmth,
you worked Scotland's upper coast,

then the soil of Colombia
serving nature and planet,
big-picture roles in small settings,
framed and filmed on location,
meeting needs of creatures,
some afloat and hungry,
or remote with quiet needs
on disconnected shores.

The Socially Distant Bird

Do birds chase lonely routes at random,
or follow deep designs from elsewhere?
Old notions say they flock to gather
with their feathered brethren. But think
how often we see them in pursuit of nothing special,
hastening flaps in point-to-point,
"as the crow flies," to express directness,
in terms of another old notion.
What sends them on their curious courses—
giddy spontaneity in naked air?
Or a circuit-driven mission,
ordering travel with a cause?
A varied aviary flies to the cardboard plate
we've nailed to a plumeria bough,
a backyard stop for flitting nibblers.
They land and peck but rarely linger
to share their gourmet comments
on papaya seeds and melon rinds,
or chunks of pear and apple cores
we set for them to sample.
Something in the wings' directness
and the forward darting bills
spells an edge of urgent aim,
rushing to escape a threat of cloudy shadows,
dark with a rumbling of thunderous energies.
The bird must know what it's flying through,
or from or toward, in a zippy silhouette,
wasting no time in island chatter,
anxious as a refugee from arising tyranny.

One thinks of other humans writing birds:
Poe and his raven, Stevens and his 13-way blackbird,
Shelley's skylark and more committed others
like TranstrØmer's migratory swallow
flying six compulsive weeks each April
from Transvaal to a barn in Europe.
Or consider Lady Dilhorne's World War pigeons,
hauling coded messages across the channel
to and from her home in Oxfordshire.
What some may think to be blithe spirits,
high on their own freedom, could be wired
for direction, trained like the rainbow doves
to fly up and away at the start of road races
and ordained to find their way back
to their coveys and coops.
Even the most gregarious bird
may cherish distance, wanting space,
sensing inner needs to flee,
or pursue alone what it's called to seek.
Grim morbidity takes an airborne twist:
"In the end you <u>fly</u> alone."

Delicate Balances

Doing a curvy lurk
in striking attraction mode,
the Pitcher Plant seems open
to the business of enticement.
Those ants may sense they're stalking a banana,
unaware how close they crawl
toward a last act without encore
inside this cloaked yellow carnivore.
The plant is not called the Nepenthes
for nothing, drawing on classical words
for a mercy-killing drug,
numbing victims from their grief
before the pain arrives.

Insinuating cobra envy
with a splash of seahorse float,
the hooded killer teases
our unwilling belief in suspension,
a Newton-defying pause
in mid-delivery perhaps,
(no elevation dysfunction here)
to notice those ants on base,
and lure the wandering bugs
to a sticky point of no return,
fatalities of its selective appetite.

The vessel of death looms forth,
clad in the color of sun,
looping out at a mobile angle

with what has the look
of a safety hook sprouting
from the back of its head.
The delicate posture somehow
of a regal bug-trapping plant,
stalls gravity with a ballet stance
of balance and poise,
one leg reaching forward,
the other back in an Arabesque,
a dance term for awkward diplomacy,
robing differences in shifting worlds,
equal parts sand, faith and oil,
a toxic oasis tempting to insects
or fooling a careless player.

How symbolic, this lethal plant,
garbed in yellow vestments, shows
its mission waiting with matador patience,
head shielded as in a welder's mask,
conditioned by nature for a terminal
path of seductive surprise.
Its errant victims find too late
their misjudgment of farewell
from a siren's serpent disguise.

How quickly nature dances from
feel-good to fatal in a moment's pivot:
a wrong choice of crosswalks,
a last glass of wine, one for the road,
served from a pitcher.

Pitchers and pictures have values,
this one worth scores of small lives,
maybe more than 1,000 words,
as a bug-hungry hit-plant
leveling nature's supply,
kinder than Raid or Black Flag,
leaving for birds and lizards,
more fast-food bites between meals.

Life grasps for a balance of planet
that keeps us looking, leaning,
reaching to hold on and share
our common polar tilting in mid-air.

The Milk of Human Gratitude

I can't pin down the quote from the author who said
he wrote for the same reasons cows give milk.
Too literally, that conceit suggests the pressure
on his back and shoulders was not just an editor's deadline
but the freshening intrusion of a grass-fed bull.
Some say it was George Bernard Shaw—
not the bull, but the writer comparing life's urges.

An animal on the receiving end of such creative muses
may not be troubled by writer's block
as much as a sense of Dairyland *de ja vu*.
As in I've had this milkshake before
and the flavor's always the same.
"Milk from Contented Cows" was Carnation's
slogan, no doubt from a clever ad man
touting the work of Pacific cattle
competing with Borden's Elsie
and regional favorites elsewhere.

Once on a visit to Madison, we spotted
cartoonish sculptings of ornate cows
positioned as smiling statues about the capital
of a state where so much depends on lactating cows,
a lifted phrase seeming more at home
than as prescribed in Dr. Williams' red wheelbarrow.

A college roommate held our attention with tales
of his self-sufficient prep school
where work on its farm was part of the deal,

he describing hygenic preparations
for milking in details you don't want to know,
in ways only teen minds could relish.
How drinkable milk survived the nearness
of barn-floor droppings could challenge
a drinker's faith in Louis Pasteur.

Even a thirsty child could lose taste for a product
splashing from a tin-pail context encroached
by a parallel flow of bodily offal,
but somehow we've all survived,
including the calves of busy mothers,
unable to feed their young while working,
some filling side bottles to meet their production.

Why a cow gives milk is a system that works
either because of or despite chained responses
more complex than that author's attempts
to link himself with the forces of nature.

Farmers now pretend to be bulls, wearing horned costumes
to get Bossy in the mood for their arm's length *in vitro*
plantings without the usual back-door romance,
though rough, still reminiscent to the bovine mind
of why that milk keeps flowing.

Another writer might tell you he stays alive
because cows give milk, but he'd have a different story.
A blood-thinner patient, he'd tell you his pill
owes its start to some Dairyland fortunes
feeding Madison's labs of science
that found the clotting cure

in a substance that poisons rats,
sold in drug stores as WARFarin,
its acronym not many know stands
for Wisconsin Alumni Research Fund.

Seagulls

Seagulls bring the force of hunger
on their wings and beaks arriving
nearly everywhere to sense a watery world
of possibilities in fish and random bites
of other edibles no human at the moment wants.
I've come to watch them poised and swooping
with the decades, but never here, because...

They dove into the Hudson, then rose straight up,
bills with their clench of wriggling dinner,
maybe perch or shad, creatures from a toxic river
where we used to swim until our elders told us
we might live in wheelchairs from its germs.
Seagulls tasted dirty rivers but not Hawai'i, because...

Off Maine's Atlantic points, their guiding presence
was a postcard must of ocean sounds
and the salted fragrance of its shoreline,
but never made the scene in Hawai'i, because...

Unlike beaches and quahog sites
en route to Narragansett and Newport,
their screech and flapping are never seen in Hawai'i, because...

On summer's Cape with its sun, sand, crowds
and whiffs of shriveled fried clams in crusty batter,
gulls seemed enthralled and hovered on docks
and breezed-grassy paths to the beaches,
but their appetites for pricey seasides
never lured them to Hawai'i, because...

At Fisherman's Wharf, they eyed the walking crab and lobster takeout trays, plastic-forked and nibbled by browsers along the seafood promenade of snacking tourists, but nothing like this in Hawai'i, because...

In Aberdeen, pre-dawn seagull shrieking
was a wake-up serenade, escorting boats
of Icelandic fish, heralding fresh-caught triumph
hauled in overnight for morning-market sales,
but even at Oahu's busy seafood auction,
you will not find a seagull anywhere, because...

At Coos Bay, seagulls found a pier-based cannery,
where human clean-cook-cut-pack discard
broadcast an all-gulls-could eat buffet to the Oregon air,
though not in Hawai'i, because...

Years of water-edge places for seafood drew gulls beyond measure:
Boston's floating ship at Pier IV, and waterfront Southwest D.C.,
with boat-side Chesapeake shelled treasures for drive-by Capitol
birds of the Hawk & Dove habits.
But nowhere to be found in Hawai'i, because...

And later, Key West, along open sandy water's strand and on posts
at Mallory Square, seafood restaurants everywhere, grifting Florida
gulls abound.
Still no presence in Hawai'i, because...

Farther in from coastal waters, in southern California, note the
seagulls scouting out the fast-food Dumpsters© in the shopping
centers, but not in commercial Hawai'i, because...

Seagulls stand in patient gray-white mode
on widespread rocks and cribbings
but not in Hawai'i.
They never made it here, because
the flight's too far to tempt them
from their land-dependent habits,
so we're told, and our depth of life
in the sea swims beyond reach
of their scavenger tastes.

Instead, we have albatross, petrels,
terns, frigate birds, boobies and noddies,
and shearwaters, named for Newell and others,
at work in the chase, gliding patrols
of the sea-tops in search of Pacific
Island waterfront dining.

We've done without our haunting gulls
but recognize their presence from a distance,
in the way of absent friends and parted family,
hoping they gather and soar like creatures of faith,
alive in our memories, awaiting us elsewhere.

Of Birds and Behavior

Birds in our backyard are always hungry.
They do not sit on utility wires,
because our lines are all underground.
They seem to like branches of trees,
depths of bushes and edges of roofs
when they loiter about to be fed
human-fixed meals, such as they are,
on plumeria limbs five feet above lawn.

Our birds do not lurk in groups,
as though waiting for sinister signals
from Alfred Hitchcock and film crew.
Cues to attack the hands that feed
are not in their mind-script, or so we think.
They scatter when they sense us
watching them through sliding glass,
pecking and gulping, snaring and snacking,
spurring stealth on our part to spy
flying traffic to the see-through cylinder
holding gourmet store-bought seeds,
a yellow-brown-gray random mosaic
of grain in the making, seeping
out of its hanging mini-silo
into a narrow-ledge tray encircling,
just right for Brazilian cardinals and Java rice birds
but a gravity challenge for eager pigeons
to balance themselves in wing-flapping frenzies
while pushing their senior gray weight around
to get theirs and scatter loose seeds

to the ground for their juniors turf-nibbling below.
Waiting their turns at the swinging feeder,
other birds sample our kitchen remnants
in a plastic tray next branch over—
apple cores, kiwi fruit skins, papaya seeds,
melon rinds, lumps of stale sourdough
and pineapple cuttings.

The minds and tastes of birds are not
so easy to read as some experts say.
Can they really smell food from a distance?
However birds learn, they arrive
as though called to a meeting.
After food's gone, they fly somewhere else.
Our meals are not served on schedule.
How do birds sense when they're waiting
alone or in groups beyond contact?

In yesterday's *Times* I read of the *Umwelt*,
of animal minds, the ranges of message and sense
that motivate motions of creatures
in ways we research but only they understand.
Some of them already know
where we stash the seed bag,
and perch on tables nearby
leaving their insider calling cards
to remind us, perhaps, of their organic presence,
as they learn to read our world,
dropping clues that link us in common.

Turtle Independence

Turtles get the survival prize,
no matter how much or little we help them,
or spoil them with hotel pool-service
or quarrel in cultural wars among humans
about whether eating them is a sin
against those popular menu items:
sustainability, resilience, regeneration.
Turtles it seems can check off all three,
but they carry ancestral flavors that tempt
ceremonial tastes of Pacific islanders.
Every July 4th, scientists, spiritual chanters,
tourists, politicos, TV camera crews gather
to free a small cohort of green turtles,
carefully kept for months in salty pools
of the Big Island's Mauna Lani Hotel.
The praying and playing of conch shells
precedes the gentle procession of humans
bearing small stretchers with turtles aboard
and bound for their ocean births,
complete with new names in Hawaiian,
a baptismal touch for the start
of new life in the waves.
Protecting them in the hotel pools
multiplies ocean survival odds by 250,
native hotel scientist "Turtle Man" tells us,
and yet these *Honu* have been here
for millions of years, we're also assured,
predating those predatory short-termers
whose tall bones now take up space in museums.

How strange the beachfront pageant
to their protection has made humans
feel better for 33 years, keeping today's
island cultures alive on the civilized map
volcanically forming with the surf of now
and the undercurrents of then.
Hawaiians were at home with metaphors,
a guide with deep island roots tells us,
their early unwritten language layered
in meanings that took outsiders a while to grasp.
Honu, the world for turtle, seems akin
to *honua*, a term meaning land or the Earth.
We're told early islanders saw a map of the Earth
in the hexagonal shapes of the turtles' shell markings.

Malama Honu means care for the turtles,
as *Malama Honua*, means care for our island Earth.
Turtles could be the ones teaching survival
that human helpers are trying to learn.

Evolving Boundaries

Evolving grows its derivative paths
through forms and classes and orders
few of us are ready to recognize,
as life latches onto the unrelated
over years of gradual shifts in appearance.

We dreamed once in time of unicorns,
sequined in mythical moonlight,
but instead awoke to the platypus,
a duck-billed creature at home in the mud
of the seas in the hemisphere south.

Are any prepared for the merging of species,
amalgams of plant and animal life,
errant survivors of flora and fauna entwined?
Alien kingdoms may indulge in new
patterns of marriage-bed mergings,
hatching worlds of unevenly modified creatures,
where ontogeny and phylogeny
lose their ways on a recap spree—*hey, hey,*
'pitulating the night away!

Consider the alarms of conglomerate beings
to those shocked by arrival of unplanned life
in suburban streets in the form of wild pigs
down from woods on the ridges in search
of their next meals and stage of survival,
a phase that might lead them downtown.

Emerging life forms may add serpent tongues
to beaks of harsh birds, or wings
to a crocodile's quiver of frights.
Our senses may not adjust well
to hybrid gyrations of foreign contours
in land-to-sea transforms bursting
from splits in each other's cell walls,
expanding life functions, adapting
to quirks in the hydrogen-oxygen ratio.

Atoms under the power of a leveling sun
with its unstoppable speed of light,
may demand new roles of the living
in ways that bypass Darwin's notes
to redraft the *Origin of Species*
en route to horizons of fear,
beyond mushroom clouds but closer
to their baby life models taking shape
with fangs in the peace of damp darkness.

Talking Turkey

Thanksgiving's a reward to sacrifice
celebrating survival with others,
not always with cheer or food at the table,
and sometimes in ways too strange to report.
Work that day in '61 scheduled a football game photo
for reasons still unclear in a mind
of many puzzles and mazes of decades,
but with his 4 x 5 Graflex he found the mayor
and his Turkish guests in the stands at the 50-yard line.
A delegation of traveling Turks
attending a Turkey Day Classic,
feeling American vibes
of a high schools sports battle
in traditional New England.
"These men are from Turkey,"
said Cranston's cautious mayor,
a year into his upset first term.
"Be careful if you quote them.
You read about the hangings, right?"
Indeed, a photo and clever word-play
caption would do the trick.
But the three of them gave him their cards
with hotel numbers he called the next day
for afternoon drinks on a quiet Friday.
Interpreted talk was friendly
among him and three 40ish Turks
with his wife along to meet them and listen.
Capital punishment was an issue he'd
covered first-hand in Ohio where its live

wires of interest were current and real,
(one jolting instance he'd witnessed himself,)
but a topic passé in humane Rhode Island,
a place of refuge Roger Williams settled
for outcasts from punitive Puritan Bay.
Ice finally broke on the coup and the hangings.
Takeover factions let most of their captives
live on in acquittal or jail,
but Prime Minister Adnan Menderes
and two of his leaders had died on the rope
only two months before.
Um, how did they feel about this?
As part of Turkey's new in-group,
they did not rejoice but gazed
in a unison straight-faced acceptance,
one adding the deaths were not done in public,
but handled swiftly in-house with dispatch,
using rafters, desktops and kicked-away chairs.
Friendly good-byes sealed the tone of their meeting,
and this seems the first ever written about it.

Beyond the tired namesake cliché
shared by a nation of curious allies
and another's historic feast bird,
(grimly humored in White House pardons,)
lives of we table guests seemed linked
in separate worlds of loss and history,
both mixtures of falsehood and faith,
served with the gravity of trust,
helpings of patience on trial,
and mutual suspensions of judgment.

AT THE CORNER OF GOOD TIMES AND TWILIGHT:

THE ANGELS ARE IN THE DETAILS

Medicine Shoulders the Burden

Smooth-soled shoes and wet concrete
put my left arm in a sling
to heal the purple shoulder's
poked-out broken humerus
spreading green, deep blue,
black and purple across
arm and chest to the sternum
and down past forearm
to the edge of the hand.
Landing on grass
was the good news,
hydroplaned feet losing it all
but missing the backyard walkway
where skidding surface launched the fall,
while tending plants in mid-morning.

Head clear but left shoulder broken
and bent, barely able to move—
proximal separations at work here,
the bone from its glenohumeral joint
and me from the house—
Inching 15 feet to sliding screen door,
shouts to neighbors unanswered,
back-crawled into house through
open door, unable to lift or move
forward on parquet floor.
More shouts to neighbors,
most at work or beyond earshot.
Miracle happenstance saved

seven hours' wait on the floor
for working wife to come home!
Neighbor's daughter drove in early
at noon, heard my shouts for help.
Her 9-1-1 call brought ambulance rescue.
Up on a gurney and into a truck,
sirens sounding to lead the way
through Wednesday noon freeway traffic
to an overcrowded medical center,
busy with routine pandemic pandemonium.
Emergency room beehive stirred to high frenzy
in 24/7 potential catastrophe mode.
Gurneys of patients form corridor gridlock.
Somehow I'm wheeled into a temp room
across from Central Nursing's nexus nerveland
with radio calls arriving from ambulance drivers
orders and signals from rooms everywhere.
Screens of reporting occupy nurses and techs.
Hospital beds were scarce long before Covid
added its land rush for room space.
ER timing has its own sequence.
Aide viewing screen reads off meds I don't take
until we discover another patient, nearly same-named,
is not me, so time to start over with input of data.
Blood thinner reading is high, so cut the Warfarin.
Fentanyl's holding off pain, Oxycodone's warming
in the bullpen in case we need more.

Ordered CPAP mask, not sure staff can find one.
Time to move, a nurse advises, pushing my gurney
out of the curtained room and into a gurney-packed
double parked route of zig-zagged table-strewn hallways,

arriving in quiet, side alcove of curtained-off spaces.
Papers exchanged among new and old handlers.
"Sorry, we have to move you back,"
the last handler returns with a crazy laugh;
this room can't take CPAP plug-ins.
Return trip angling bumper-car style through gurneys,
racks, and tables on wheels, back to Room 22 where we started,
blue-suited aide laughing all the way.
Other trips for X-rays and CAT scan, plastic bottle
in tow to soothe my busy bladder,
and back to the room for overnight rest.
CPAP showed up to link sleep with oxygen dreams.

Mealtime surprise has its place on the menu,
kitchen schedules preempting the others;
breakfast wheels in unannounced as we're
easing away from a freshly-filled bed pan.
The food is good, by the way, though
last among things on my mind.

A bell somewhere sounded *ding-ding-ding* like an alarm stuck for
    minutes.
Nurses and techs continued to work as though no one heard it.
No one sees my waving arms, bell button not reconnected after
    recent visit.
With cellphone I dialed the ER switchboard to ask what's going on.
"What room are you in?" a voice asked.
"Twenty-two," I answered, minutes before a nurse showed up.
"Sorry, I was busy elsewhere," she said, finding a switch
    to turn off the dinging, which no one but I had heard for an hour.

Late Thursday a room opened up on a tower top floor eight stories
　　above,
many corridor turns and two elevator rides away.
Far from the chaos of intake, troubled patients crying,
"Nurse!," "Help me!," "Is anyone here?," and "Where am I?"
　were new sounds to break the calm contrast.
Call-button use was a skill they had not acquired,
or one they feared wouldn't work.
"Where is your sling?" was a question I often was asked.
On Friday a sling showed up, a blue off-the-shelf garment,
one-size-fits-none, a therapist taught me to arm, adjust and remove.

"No, thanks," I said to the Oxycodone—I'd been there before
and survived toilet pains only polyethylene glycol could ease,
but Tylenol allowed me to sleep, until awakened at night
by a sweet-whispered voice of a nurse taking blood pressure.
In the dark she cuffed the upper arm of my broken humerus,
squeezing air tightly onto my greenish black bicep, then slipped
　　away in the night.
The pressure read 181, a new nurse a few minutes later reported,
this time cuffing the uninjured right arm and getting a 171.
"Pain can affect your readings," she said,
leaving me and my startled BP to recover.

Hospital care was hectic but good,
not a place to look for perfection,
with all hands on deck and nurses
from elsewhere pressed into duty,
shock troops deployed at the ready,
it's a wonder the health help survives,
let alone patients, just mostly confused.
The bill for it all cost me $10,
a bargain, no doubt, for a three-day co-pay.

A hospital doctor said shoulder surgery seemed unneeded.
My own doc said the break would self-heal.
The orthopod showed me X-rays of bones still apart.
Keep surgery on the table, he said. I might need it.
Odds of self-healing are 80 per cent, he agreed.
But this might be a job for knives and pins
to restore full use of left shoulder.
His X-rays showed space between the humerus top
and neighboring bones near the socket.
Decision is mine, the ortho doc says, but keep options open.
At 86, I ponder the trade-off—full use vs. more hospital time
and back to One Recovery Square, an address I'd like to avoid.
The healing question's still open, like the space between bones
and the doctors' separate opinions.

Tongue-tied by a TIA

Trying to talk and suddenly
not being able hit me
one December night
when I wanted to answer my wife.
Not the marriage joke it might sound like:
I waited for seconds to pass
then formed a parade of my thoughts
and slowly began their procession,
breathing slowly, as each word
stepped forth as intended.
Conversation quickly regained
its usual hectic cadence,
but I took note and brought
it up to her later, we both agreeing
it should be reported.
Turns out it was a TIA—
a Transient Ischemic Attack.
Just to be sure, doctor put me
through a brain and a CAT scan
to see if this mini-stroke symptom
arose from more plaque
caking in the carotid.
Some, he said, but not serious.
For a blood-thinner patient
with cholesterol worries,
this kind of thing needs
keeping track of, he said,
and continue those statins.
To my medical namedrops

I added the term TIA
after training my tongue
to pronounce it correctly—
not isthmus, not isthemic, not ischial,
but ischemic, as in ischemia,
a shortage of oxygen
fed by blood to heart and brain.
My being unable to speak
breathes irony into past family life.
My father loved the comic quote:
"You spend three years teaching a kid to talk
and the next 30 trying to get him to stop."
Elsewhere, TIA means Thanks in Advance,
a term I extend to those who might notice
next time I seem to be struggling for words.

Blue Roses

Can flowers that glow like blue roses
survive to celebrate feelings that last?
Reluctant to order 80 of them
for someone whose years match the number,
though greater in color and strength,
more vibrant of purpose in loyal array,
lasting beyond duty hours
when others around her have faded
against a sun that wilts its rivals
with firebursts of mission-despair.

Blue roses draw a planet's own
solar message of envy,
an unyielding gold drive
overpowering stems that cast
explosions of joy and regret
to determined hearts.
Blue roses show forth as reflected
contrivance of sea and sky,
unmirrored in nature's supply.

Artists and petal-dye florists
can bring them to life for moments
on display with measured effect,
a stoic awareness shared
in the startle of heaven's appeal.

Science tries at growing them blue,
but has little to show for its magic,
experiments finding deep purple,
an easier stripe of the rainbow
to pull from the ground
through green shoots to buds
raising only colors of bruise
to their blossoming petals.

That chorus of 80 in blue
beyond lab test-tube's reach
may gather their ranks in formation
to stand tall, salute or fly by
(though neither confirm nor deny)
her *Octobergenarian* birthday.

They might pose in virtual display,
but their brief glories
yield to her outshining force
whose impact exceeds sea and sky,
plus powers of sun and Earth
to flower a rose of her brightness.

At 80 and Looking Forward

Our *Octobergenarian*'s a life force with outreach
that sounds like it fits the month of her birth:
all the fish in the sea cannot count
places her attentive tentacles touch
with unfurling direction and care.
The deep caves of work among
surface tides and undercurrents
family worries for young, old and mid-life
in distant states of success and distress,
island family issues spreading
to uncertain creatures in transition,
shuffling riddles in lives and work
or life's horizon points shifting.
Eight decades deliver wisdom
but concerns as well that late years
part ways with earlier dreams.
Suspicion reacts to contact points
which once were sources of joy,
and truth may feed back with remorse.
What realities await a busy course that charts
new paths away from the happy album pages,
the spirited lore of a Hallowe'en birth
lighting the future from wartime dark?
All past postcards of smiling hope
now seem to set tones for passing waves
of fading might-have-beens.
Hard work and unlimited sharing
bright days with the lonely,
connecting others' loose ends

with rescuing grasps of concern's
tough affection may total less
than her view of the future expected.
How to reckon seas of ambition
with inlets and coves of closing results
becomes a new test for life after 80,
a time when those you've guided
and trusted may be less in their finish
than those you'd sought to include
in life-spreading arms of assistance.
How to make these new fought-for years
times to rest and extend to new interests
the care and strength you still have
for a longer life blest among those
of us gratefully hoping to share it
and trying our best to deserve it.

Flowers on the Brain

Flowers celebrate
life's mortal points,
crescendos of hope allowed
to burst amid the routine
gray matters of existence,
powered as if by cerebral cells
for as long as they can.

Impermanent glories
inspire the heart but grow
from serotonin to the brain,
as we design their implants
to crest above the shoulders
and into the floral glee of the hair.

Science has found and now
sings aloud that blooms convey
endocrine warmths of brightness,
glowing us in their light, as time
deadly works to outlast us.

Wreaths of needle-strung petals,
bright *lei*, rise to eye level
and decorate youth's happy plateaus,
while silk-sashed altar sprays,
larger than life-cycle tires,
halos in waiting on A-frame display,
say farewell at the end.

For blossoming joy
in this world or the next,
"flowers on the brain"
seems a condition worth growing,
contagious in its appeal.

Flowers on the brain
enable your seeing of kids
as too green in the bud to be judged,
while sensing most elders accept
the dry arrangements they've reached.

Flowers on the brain
regard the red hibiscus
profusing as blood spurts of stars
afloat in a green-leaf sky,
watered each night at their roots
from a hose that jets torrents—
a self-fulfilling dowser
adding lordly thrust
to divining-rod faith—
aiming life force at roots
where powers of growth
receive delivered wonders
from florally-active voices
shouting of regeneration.

Hard Edges

Through cracks in the pavement
life proceeds against odds,
to the semi-awareness of jogger-walkers
learning paved patterns of roadwork
and seeing what blooms in unlikely seams
along a route of keeping the mind in focus
on the next step, the heart on the coming beat.

A Tree Grows in Brooklyn, my father explained,
was titled to show a child emerging
among the hard blocks and worn stairs,
the concrete resistance of city life,
to overcome years of family despair.
The '40s best seller grew roots in the mind,
though Betty Smith's life was different,
surely a far place from mine,
still just 30 miles south on the map,
its story reminding millions of hope
and persistence linked like blossom and root.

The ground is hard in other lands,
and many pursue the seeking of life
within Earth's fickle surfaces.
A daughter in her 60s (and of the '60s)
has tried her hand at growing the spirit
of climate concern on three continents
and now returns to Colombia
where a non-profit effort goes forth
to make the soil grow more than plans for resorts.

She has paid her dues as parent and pastor
and now keeps trying to flower small causes
to encourage the Earth and safeguard its living
from a spot on the globe called Barichara.

A son now 50 grew and shared corn
in the hard-to-please dirt of North Texas,
but his second-round crop was no match
for bugs and fungus, showing nature
has enemies of its own, superseding cement.

Another daughter, late 40s, is off to Brazil
sowing some of the billions her boss's
foundation invests in climate-care grants.
At home, her daughters, 14 and 10, grow
quickly in their uphill sidewalk Bay city,
neighbors' yards open markets of cactus
and other less-watered plants on display
with what seems like minimal care.

Hollyhocks come to mind as rising
to bright colored petals, tall stems
with big leaves all determined
to sprout where they like, not a surprise
to see them command the hard corners,
where walkways meet asphalt.

Here, where everything grows as in Eden,
avocados can leap from their seedpits,
placed in light soil and watered,
with overnight action and need
for more daily hosing than weather

can give in a land caught between
daily rainfall and drought.
Avocados take on a semblance to poems,
some appearing to flourish, deserving attention,
others with promising leaves turning brown
and meanings once-green that wither,
even as gardener-of-words
tries desperate hose-water rescues.

Much drifts through the distance-walker's sights,
a familiar painting of pink hearts
boldly sweeping in style on the sidewalk,
a series of five beside a stone church
near the stoplight corner. What, one wonders,
led someone with a brush to splash
giant Valentines in such a place?

The five-of-hearts means
nothing special in most card games
but is seen as good news in Tarot.
The pedestrian oddity is not lost
amid the walker's thoughts
of his flowering family
and a life that continues,
extending each day
among hard edges
in tightening space.

Features of Death

Faces of our early dead
emerge in dreams as they shone
early on—office-bright,
yearbook-young—residual joy
a part of our partial recall.
But faces now before us
from the recent older dead
surface in layered remembrance
of gradual phases, canvas-textured,
mummified in archival honor,
taking on a sculptured golden look
of polished brass in *bas-relief*
on their Hall-of-Fame smiles,
monoliths in a stadium outfield sun.

Or from the assemblage
of strips of *papier-mache'*
visages of the old come forth
as achievements of surface,
appearing for a haunting cameo
perhaps on a Christmas door-knocker,
a morphing ghost of partners past,
a father figure visage now reflected
in an aging son's mirrored wrinkles
portraying yet another
generation's sudden sense
of the masked inevitable.

Lenin in his airtight Red Square casket
lies sealed for viewing with unchanged face,
somewhat like St. John XXIII in Rome.
Lesser creatures in uncovered states
show mannequins of final looks,
some puffy, darker, blank or grim.
Family members arrayed for viewing
seem re-sleeping their terminal days,
times we recall as carved in pain,
maybe more ours than theirs.
Eyes that link lives fuse our thoughts.
Deep gazes are what we extend
to rekindle a final joining,
to look into and beyond
those sundowned faces
for closing flashes of light.

About Time

Quality time shouldn't wait till it's lost
in the hour glass and has to be rationed.
Who decides when and how time earns its labels?
Like the Michelin Guide on places to eat
or J.D. Power's ratings of cars?
We spend billions on gadgets and links
designed to learn secret codes of time
in order to save it—to store it in cloudy vaults
to hold for other needs —until techs find ways
to obsolesce those with more mashing of digits,
stretching seconds to make them longer
slicing nanos to make more of them.
Does time saved top time spent
on quality's leader board standings?
An aging writer rushes to keyboard
to share wit with a Zoom screen
of friends he hopes will remember.
Does that effort outrank
in the uses of time
a quiet card to a distant kin?
Driving home, he sees the ridges,
looming shadowed pillars edged
and cut as muscled stone
from dry-weathered bronze,
now a darkening holiday green,
an afternoon sketched in winter's sun,
site of a weekend's wind-driven rain,
destructive to some but craved by others,
said to be good for what needs us

and for what _we_ need _for_ us as well,
the hills of the Earth and their trees.
Were the hours we shivered indoors
to outwait the storm *quality time,*
as it was for athletes with boards
balancing skills on windy gray waves?
Time reappraises itself as it fades,
rear-viewing the past as chances missed,
pitfalls dodged, turning points marked,
its *quality* trait the speed of its passing.
A traveling father ends a holiday visit
with a time-sharing daughter,
he en route to his waiting car.
Bye, Daddy. See you again sometime.
At 62 now, she's had her own sad moments,
but those farewell words have echoed
a half-century's time-travel haunting to him.
The once-little girl breaks her Earth-saving mission
for holiday time with her senior-care Mom
in the frozen Midwest, *a quality time*
that melts part of a personal ice age.
Time seems to seek its own value level.
Would *quality time* have more worth
if it punched a clock to herald its presence?
And if it did, would we welcome it
with both our big and little hands?

Command of the Language

"...and the Word was God." John 1:1

The word is fleeing its bindings,
facts and numbers not far behind.
Watch as the blocks where writers
lived in crumpled frustration
melt down in electrified codings and couplings
re-emerging on screen in narrative life
as the organized text your mind,
mouth and hands once worked
with care and pride to deliver.

Our shelves of books from the past
make scenic backdrops in studies
and historic rooms, bequeathing
legacies in warmed red-brown vertical glow,
ceiling to floor in a towering corduroy
of gilt-edged wisdom beckoning all
to their massive remoteness of treasure.
The magnificent masterpiece looks
are no longer needed as cathedrals of faith
to back up the instant prayer so many use,
almost as 9-1-1 dialing to answer
the needs of the moment,
the right words for today.

The flight of word continues
beyond the books of knowledge,
updated World Almanacs,
five-foot collections,

the doorstep encounters
demanding full family attention
for lifetime commitments
to Brittanica's system of learning,
the hard-covered Queen Mother
of Alpha to Omega.
Words may celebrate decolonizing
from encyclopedic empires, dictionary dictates,
the tyranny of Thesaurus Rex,
and the oligarchs of originality.

Now words are free to mingle
in random digital rendezvous,
dancing about and coming together,
as though in a syllabic singles bar,
regrouping elsewhere at the suggestion
of a few smart lines.
The bindings words have fled
are also those of the owners
of elegant books and their words,
writers esteemed in décor,
but needed only to sign their work
as having been theirs—or almost
—as many may start to get by
with a little help from the bots of A.I.

Too Late for Sweet Sorrows

Don't look now, but hand-in-hand
we're scaling the mountains together.
Looking back lends a last frame
as we leave the treetops forever,
ridges fading from green to brown
and back to green to greet others
whose time and hopes continue,
as they follow in valleys below us,
moving uphill, gently at first
then gaining ground all of a sudden.
Joined in memories of closing flesh,
we try to resist the pursuit,
destiny faltering somewhere between
Wait! what? and *This thing is real.*
Sharing quiet alarms of reluctance,
we leave the beaches of joy,
rise from the traffic of work,
abandon parades of life purpose.

Don't look back, but they're going
their way, as we're going ours
on a quick route bypassing the light
we'd thought we might share
to match our own brightness.
That Golden Age glow we linked
to achieve has cooled in reflection,
as now we proceed beyond skyline
wondering how much we'll mean
to those advancing through hillsides
of trails, soon to recede from our view
and we, without waving, from theirs.

Memorial Day Lights

(Six haiku)

Honolulu HI

Floating flames display
memories for those we miss,
one May night each year.

Asian hosts deploy
top star brass on jumbo screens
to soothe wars' mournings.

Shinnyo-en has launched
"Many Rivers, One Ocean"
for two decades now.

Grieving prompts this rare
time we flicker waves to care
for lost lives we share.

Candle floats retrieved,
hushed thousands leave sea beach park,
in dark reflection.

High-rise windows glow
nearby, towered lights of lives
we may never know.

Short-listed

Tomorrows keep coming,
thanks to prayer,
plans and wishes.
The revolution of time
and nature continues
rotating patterns of force,
affirming forces of pattern.

The paper in our driveway confirms
what we saw yesterday
really took place, validating
that time turns its pages,
displaying the dates,
as though proof of life
in a ransom demand,
holding hostage our hopes for return.

One son dead, another's lone kidney
hanging on in need of a match,
a younger brother gone to cancer,
another stoic in survival,
alone in the winter of life.

Who are tomorrow's companions
when survival reaches Stage 4
in a process of elimination,
life promises blown flameless
as candles on yesterday's icing?

Morning print unfolds
to reveal that those whose
passing lives we learn of
cannot read with us
about themselves today,
the tomorrow that came too late
for them to celebrate
and share our hope for another.
They add new reasons
to work for the priceless dawn
we pray and sleep to greet tomorrow,
one day closer to forever.

Acknowledgements

Three poems in this collection have appeared, or been chosen for inclusion, in other publications for which grateful appreciation is acknowledged.

The Socially Distant Bird was published in *In a Roundabout Way,* by John E. Simonds, Dorrance Publishing Co., Pittsburgh PA, in 2021.

Short-Listed was published in the San Francisco Writers Conference 2021 Writing Contest Anthology, New Alexandria Creative Group, San Francisco CA, in 2021.

Medicine Shoulders the Burden has been accepted for publication in the 45th Anniversary edition, issue #124 of *Bamboo Ridge,* Honolulu HI, in 2023.

Many thanks also to regional literary groups in Honolulu, Los Angeles, San Francisco, Chicago, Telluride CO, Houston and Plano TX for their encouragement via online sharing and open mic readings during and after the coronavirus months of isolation.

About Atmosphere Press

Atmosphere Press is an independent, full-service publisher for excellent books in all genres and for all audiences. Learn more about what we do at atmospherepress.com.

We encourage you to check out some of Atmosphere's latest releases, which are available at Amazon.com and via order from your local bookstore:

Melody in Exile, by S.T. Grant

Covenant, by Kate Carter

Near Scattered Praise Lies Our Substantial Endeavor, by Ron Penoyer

Weightless, Woven Words, by Umar Siddiqui

Journeying: Flying, Family, Foraging, by Nicholas Ranson

Lexicon of the Body, by DM Wallace

Controlling Chaos, by Michael Estabrook

Almost a Memoir, by M.C. Rydel

Throwing the Bones, by Caitlin Jackson

Like Fire and Ice, by Eli

Sway, by Tricia Johnson

A Patient Hunger, by Skip Renker

Lies of an Indispensable Nation: Poems About the American Invasions of Iraq and Afghanistan, by Lilvia Soto

The Carcass Undressed, by Linda Eguiliz

Poems That Wrote Me, by Karissa Whitson

Gnostic Triptych, by Elder Gideon

For the Moment, by Charnjit Gill

Battle Cry, by Jennifer Sara Widelitz

I woke up to words today, by Daniella Deutsch

Never Enough, by William Guest

Second Adolescence, by Joe Rolnicki

About the Author

John Simonds, a retired Honolulu daily newspaper editor, has lived with his family in Hawai'i for more than 45 years and previously was a reporter for newspapers from Washington, D.C., and other cities. A Bowdoin College graduate and former east coast and midwest resident, he has been writing poems since the 1970s, including three previous collections, *Waves from a Time-Zoned Brain* (AuthorHouse 2009), *Footnotes to the Sun* (iUniverse 2015), and *In a Roundabout Way* (Dorrance 2021). He has been involved in the Hawai'i Literary Arts Council, Friends of the East-West Center, and distance-jogging (now walking) events with the Mid-Pacific Road Runners Club. He and his wife, Kitty, have children and grandchildren in WI. TX and CA, and many nieces, nephews and in-laws in Hawai'i.